34 95

Rigor Is NOT a Four-Letter Word

Second Edition

Barbara R. Blackburn

Routledge
Taylor & Francis Group

LONDON AND NEW YORK

First Published 2012 by Eye On Education

Published 2013 by Routledge
2 Park Square, Milton Park, Abingdon, Oxon OX14 4RN
711 Third Avenue, New York, NY, 10017, USA

Routledge is an imprint of the Taylor & Francis Group, an informa business

Library of Congress Cataloging-in-Publication Data

Blackburn, Barbara R., 1961–
Rigor is not a four-letter word/Barbara R. Blackburn.—Second edition.
     pages   cm
ISBN 978-1-59667-226-0
1. Education, Secondary—Aims and objectives—United States.
2. Motivation in education—United States.
3. Educational change—United States.
4. High schools—Curricula—United States.
5. High school graduates—Employment—United States.
6. College students—United States.
I. Title.
LB1607.5.B53 2012
373.01'1—dc23   2012034928

ISBN: 978-1-596-67226-0 (pbk)

Cover Designer: Dave Strauss, 3FoldDesign

Printed and bound in the United States of America by Sheridan Books, Inc. (a Sheridan Group Company).

Dedication

This book is dedicated to Abbigail, who exemplifies
the very best of what I believe about rigor.

Acknowledgments

To my family, whose encouragement is always critical. Dad, thank you for reading every chapter and making sure I made sense! Pete, you fill my life with color.

To Chad, who models rigor in his own profession and balances high expectations with humor. You always seemed to know exactly what to say.

To my friends—Katt, Shane and Jan, and Missy—thank you for your continual support.

To Ron Williamson, for his ideas, thoughts, and materials for chapter 9: Collaboration and Professional Learning Communities, thank you for your insight.

To Missy Miles and Lindsay Yearta, whose research, feedback, and creativity made a crucial difference in the quality of this book. Each of you incorporates rigor in your teaching in ways that benefit your students. You balance rigor with motivation and engagement so that your students rise to new levels of learning.

To Bob Sickles at Eye On Education, thank you for giving me the opportunity to write the book that was waiting to come to life in me.

To Allison Clark, Patricia Conner, Claudia Geocaris, Ann Linson, Barbara Moore, Gary Pankiewicz, and Debbie Shults—thank you for your suggestions, which helped me clarify and refine the content.

To Dave Strauss, you came through with your usual flair for the cover!

To Tom McCooey and Matthew Williams, thanks for the great jobs you did in copyediting and page make-up.

To Carlee Lingerfelt and Michael Sudduth for their re-creation of the musical graphic organizer in chapter 4, Increase Complexity.

Finally, to the teachers in my life, my former students, the individuals who shared their stories with me, and all those who read my books and use the ideas to impact students, thank you. You make a difference every day in the lives of your students.

Meet the Author

Dr. Barbara Blackburn has dedicated her life to raising the level of rigor and motivation for professional educators and students alike. What differentiates Barbara's 12 books are her easily executable concrete examples based on decades of experience as a teacher, professor, and consultant. Barbara's dedication to education was inspired in her early years by her parents, Bob and Rose. Her father's doctorate and lifetime career as a professor taught her the importance of professional training. Her mother's career as school secretary shaped Barbara's appreciation of the effort all staff play in the education of every child.

Barbara has taught early childhood, elementary, middle, and high school students and has served as an educational consultant for three publishing companies. She holds a master's degree in school administration and is certified as a teacher and school principal in North Carolina. She received her PhD in Curriculum and Teaching from the University of North Carolina at Greensboro. In 2006, she received the award for Outstanding Junior Professor at Winthrop University. She recently left her position at the University of North Carolina at Charlotte to write and speak full-time.

In addition to speaking at state and national conferences, she also regularly presents workshops for teachers and administrators in elementary, middle, and high schools. Her workshops are lively and engaging and filled with practical information. Her most popular topics include:

- Rigor Is NOT a Four Letter Word
- Rigorous Schools and Classrooms: Leading the Way
- Instructional Strategies That Motivate Students
- Content Literacy Strategies for the Young and the Restless
- Motivating Yourself and Others
- Engaging Instruction Leads to Higher Achievement
- High Expectations and Increased Support Lead to Success

For more information, or to contact Dr. Blackburn about a possible presentation, please visit her website: www.barbarablackburnonline.com

Table of Contents

Free Downloads

Many of the tools discussed and displayed in this book are also available on the Routledge website as Adobe Acrobat files. Permission has been granted to purchasers of this book to download these tools and print them.

You can access these downloads by visiting www.routledge.com/9781596672260 and clicking on the Free Downloads tab.

Templates

Bonus Templates:

Preface

This book began when I wrote a chapter of the same name for *Classroom Motivation from A to Z*. Although one chapter of 26, it struck a chord with teachers across the nation. Faced with the ever-increasing pressure to increase rigor in the classroom, teachers continually asked me, "How?" After five years of research, this is the answer to that question.

As I was finishing the last chapter, I was asked by one of my students, "Why do you always talk about what the teacher can do in the classroom? Why not how to change the overall educational system?" That is simple. Despite a culture that seems to devalue teachers, I still believe the most powerful change in the life of a student occurs when an individual teacher has high expectations of that student, and then acts on those expectations in ways that help the student be successful. I regularly see teachers who work in the best and the worst of situations. But I also see them making the choice to help their students be more than who they are today. And that is rigor.

The call for rigor is heard even more loudly now that we have the Common Core State Standards. This second edition of *Rigor Is Not a Four-Letter Word* puts rigor in the context of the standards and shows how the classroom activities align with the standards (see page 169). This second edition also includes new sections on problem-based learning and working with students with special needs.

My goal is for you to immediately use what you read in this book. Each chapter is organized into smaller topics. After a section of information, you'll find It's Your Turn! Space is provided for you to reflect on the concept, and immediately apply it to your specific situation.

If you are a principal, curriculum specialist, professional development coordinator, or anyone who leads professional development activities, there are resources built-in for your use. The It's Your Turn! sections throughout the text will provide discussion starters. There is an online guide for study groups and book clubs (see p. xv).

Finally, many of the templates or activity guides found throughout the book are available to you in electronic format on my website: www.barbarablackburnonline.com. You may also contact me through the site. I would like to hear from you as you implement the ideas from the book. One of my favorite parts of writing is listening to teachers and students share how they took an idea and made it their own.

1

The Case for Rigor

Introduction

I've been in education for over 25 years. I was a teacher, an educational consultant, and a professor, and now I work with teachers and administrators as a consultant. Throughout my experiences, I have learned many things from my students and from other teachers and administrators. Three of those frame my beliefs about rigor.

```
                        Lessons Learned
            ♦  Power of an Individual Teacher
            ♦  Students Reflect Our Perspectives
            ♦  Focus on What We Can Control
```

First, I have seen the power of an individual classroom teacher. My most memorable teachers were also the ones who held me to high standards. As I work with schools, I am privileged to see teachers who make a difference, even in difficult circumstances. One teacher always has made a difference in the life of a student. One teacher always will make a difference in the life of a student.

Next, I know that students reflect our perspective of them. My second year, I was assigned to teach two classes of remedial students. They came into class with a defeated, despondent attitude. In response to my enthusiasm about the upcoming year, Rhonda said, *"We know we are in the dumb class. Everyone else knows too. Didn't you know that?"* Over the course of the year, my students slowly responded to my belief that they were capable of learning. It took time, but they learned to believe in themselves, in part because I believed in them.

Finally, we should focus on the things we can control and quit worrying about those things that are out of our control. That lens served as a filter for the content of this book. With every chapter, I asked myself, *"Is this something a teacher could decide to implement in his or her classroom?"* Too often, I meet teachers who believe they have no control over anything, but that is not true. Focus on your choices. For example, you may have a student who works after school, and that prevents her from staying for tutoring at the end of the day. Rather than feeling frustrated and wishing she would miss work, offer her another option for tutoring, perhaps in the morning. When you focus on what you can control, you'll feel more productive.

The Call for Rigor

In 1983, the National Commission on Excellence in Education released its landmark report *A Nation at Risk*. It painted a clear picture: test scores were declining, lower standards resulted in American schools that were not competitive with schools from other countries, and students were leaving high school ill-prepared for the demands of the workforce. *"Our nation is at risk . . . The educational foundations of our society are presently being eroded by a rising tide of mediocrity that threatens our very future as a nation and a people."*

Over 25 years later, similar criticisms are leveled at today's schools.

New Calls for Rigor

In the four years since I wrote the original version of this book, the call for more rigor has only increased. *The Condition of College and Career Readiness*, a thorough report from the ACT, has reinforced the lack of preparedness by high school graduates for college and for the workforce.

Additionally, the focus on increased rigor has shifted to other grade ranges as well. For example, SREB's report, *Preparing Middle School Students for High School Success*, underscores the need for rigor in the middle school years:

> Many students entering the ninth grade are not prepared for the more demanding course work required of high school students—and they know it. On a 2006 survey of more than 11,000 ninth-graders at *High Schools That Work* (HSTW) schools, 39 percent of students said they were not prepared with the necessary reading skills for college-preparatory high school courses. Additionally, 49 percent reported being unprepared in writing, 57 percent reported being unprepared in mathematics and 60 percent reported being unprepared in science. (p. 1)

Finally, the new Common Core State Standards (www.corestandards .org) reinforce the need for increased rigor. Rigor is at the center of the standards, and much of the push for the standards came from a concern about the lack of rigor in many schools today, as well as the need to prepare students for college and careers (Blackburn, 2011).

Seven Myths About Rigor

Despite all the research, there are seven myths about rigor that are often heard. Let's look at each.

Seven Myths
1. Lots of homework is a sign of rigor.
2. Rigor means doing more.
3. Rigor is not for everyone.
4. Providing support means lessening rigor.
5. Resources equal rigor.
6. Standards alone take care of rigor.
7. Rigor is just one more thing to do.

Myth One: Lots of homework is a sign of rigor.

For many people the best indicator of rigor is the amount of homework required of students. Some teachers pride themselves on the amount of homework expected of their students, and there are parents who judge teachers by homework quantity. Realistically, all homework is not equally useful. Some of it is just busywork, assigned by teachers because principals or parents expect it. For some students, doing more homework in terms of quantity leads to burnout. When that occurs, students are less likely to complete homework, and may be discouraged about any learning activity.

Myth Two: Rigor means doing more.

"Doing more" often means doing more low-level activities, frequently repetitions of things already learned. Such narrow and rigid approaches to learning do not define a rigorous classroom. Students learn in many different ways. Just as instruction must vary to meet the individual needs of students, so must homework. Rigorous and challenging learning experiences will vary with the student. Their design will vary; as will their duration. Ultimately, it is the quality of the assignment that makes a difference in terms of rigor.

Myth Three: Rigor is not for everyone.

Often, teachers think the only way to assure success for everyone is to lower standards and lessen rigor. This may mask a hidden belief that some students can't really learn at high levels. You may have heard of the Pygmalion Effect—students live up to or down to our expectations of them. Each student can complete rigorous work at high levels, whether they are advanced or a student with special needs. Does the end result look different for those two students? Yes, but I know from my own experience as a teacher of struggling students reading far below their grade level that any teacher can be rigorous, and any student can reach higher levels with the right support.

Myth Four: Providing support means lessening rigor.

In America, we believe in rugged individualism. We are to pull ourselves up by our bootstraps and do things on our own. Working in teams or accepting help is often seen as a sign of weakness. Supporting students so that they can learn at high levels is central to the definition of rigor. As teachers design lessons moving students toward more challenging work, they must provide scaffolding to support them as they learn.

Myth Five: Resources equal rigor.

Recently, I've heard a common refrain. "If we buy this program, or textbook, or technology, then we would be rigorous." The right resources can certainly help increase the rigor in your classroom. However, raising the level of rigor for your students is not dependent on the resources you have. Think about the resources you have now. How can you use them more effectively? Do you use a textbook that includes true-false tests? Often, they are not rigorous because students can guess the answer. However, add one step for more rigor. Ask students to rewrite all false answers into true statements, and it requires students to demonstrate true understanding. It's not the resources; it's how you use them that make a difference.

Myth Six: Standards alone take care of rigor.

Standards alone, even if they are rigorous, do not guarantee rigor in the classroom. The Common Core State Standards are designed to increase the level of rigor in classrooms across the nation. However, if implemented without high levels of questioning or applications, the standards themselves are weakened. Your instructional practices, or how you implement standards, are just as critical as the curriculum.

Myth Seven: Rigor is just one more thing to do.

Rigor is not another thing to add to your plate. Instead, rigor is increasing the level of expectation of what you are already doing. For example, if you are teaching vocabulary, instead of asking students to write their own definition of the word, ask them to write a riddle. It's the same end result, but at higher levels of Bloom's Taxonomy.

It's Your Turn!

Which myths did you believe? What adjustments do you need to make to shift your view?

Myth	New Information That Helps Me Adjust

Another useful source of information is Cris Tovani's book, *So What Do They Really Know?* She provides a chart comparing the differences between hard and rigorous work outside of school. It is a valuable tool to consider for school also.

The Differences Between Hard and Rigorous
in the World Outside of School

Hard	*Rigorous*
Learners avoid hard tasks.	Learners embrace rigorous tasks.
The goal is the same for everyone no matter what their starting place is.	The goal changes as learners achieve small successes. With each success, a new goal is set.
Lack of success discourages learners.	Small successes keep the learners coming back for more.
Someone or something other than the learner is in control of the process and the timetable for success.	Learners have control over the process and also determine how quickly they progress.
Expectations are unreasonable because they are not set by the learner, but by outsiders who maintain control.	Expectations are set by the learner, and because the expectation is realistic, the learner sticks with the task.
Learners are frustrated because they lack tools and strategies to access the task.	Learners are empowered because they have tools and strategies to access the task.
Learners need outside prodding or extrinsic rewards to engage.	Learners prod themselves because intrinsic rewards drive them to engage.
Learners don't see a need for the task because it has no immediate relevance to their life.	Learners recognize a need for the learning and see a purpose for the work.
Compliance takes place because the performance of the task is done for someone else.	Engagement takes place because learning is for the individual.

From *So What Do They Really Know?* by Cris Tovani, Copyright © 2011, reproduced with permission of Stenhouse Publishers. www.stenhouse.com

Does This Really Matter?

You may disagree with some of the comments so far. Or, you may feel they don't apply to you. I understand. And I sympathize with the frustration of teachers who feel like everyone is telling them what to do. I heard a speaker say that education is the one profession in which everyone believes they are an expert because they have gone to school. But the reality is that we do need to increase the level of rigor in classrooms across our nation. There are schools where everyone is expected to learn at a high level and all students show growth and experience success. However, there are also many places where students, especially those who are not placed in advanced classes, are not held to high expectations.

As I continued to work with my graduate students, who were full-time teachers, as well as teachers in schools across the nation, I found myself caught in a tug-of-war of sorts. On the one hand, can anyone really argue with the notion that each student should be expected to do his or her best, learn at a maximum level, and be prepared for a future after high school that gives him or her the opportunity to be successful? On the other hand, I agree with James Beane, who said "Dictionary definitions of 'rigor' typically use terms like 'harsh,' 'inflexible in opinion,' 'severe,' and 'tyrannical.' Such terms hardly seem suitable to characterize the kinds of intellectual learning experiences we would hope young people have in our schools (NMSA, 2001)." His point reminds me of a comment from a five-year-old: "Rigor? Is that what mean teachers do?"

I was at a middle school and had a conversation with a student named Gabrielle. My favorite question to ask students is, *"If you were in charge of the school, what would you change?"* Her answer was insightful. She said, *"For people who don't understand as much . . . [they should] be in higher level classes to understand more [because] if they already don't know much, you don't want to teach them to not know much over and over."* Isn't that reflective of how students view our levels of expectations in classes that are not labeled "higher level"? Make no mistake, there is a need to increase rigor in our classrooms today.

Students' Perceptions of Rigor

As I began writing this book, I wanted to hear what students would say, since they are the ones who are most directly impacted by the decision to increase rigor in the classroom. I asked, "How do you feel about rigor, or challenging work in school?" I received over 400 responses from students in grades two through twelve. Their replies reflect that tug-of-war of negative and positive perceptions.

Students' Responses About Challenging Work

♦ I would want to quit. I would need help. *Robert*

♦ I really don't mind it. I prefer to be challenged rather than bored. *Tim*

♦ I don't like work like that because if I spend a long time on just one problem and can't find the answer I get stressed and that just makes it harder to do. *Amy*

♦ I think it's okay. I mean, I don't prefer it, but it's not as bad as most people think. Sometimes I prefer to have a little bit of a challenge. *Kyle*

♦ It makes my head and hand hurt. *Hayley*

♦ I don't like doing rigor but everything in life isn't easy so I just try my best to do it. *Dominique*

♦ I feel that rigorous work needs to be explained better than normal work so I understand the material. *Benjamin*

♦ I feel that challenging work would be better for people that think their work is too easy. *Sumerlyn*

♦ OK, but if it's hard, I want it to be fun too. *Keith*

♦ I feel that rigorous work is made for some people and some people just might get frustrated and give up. I guess everyone should at least try it and if they can't do it they don't have to. *Mason*

♦ I honestly don't mind it every once in a while but not every hour of the day. *Devon*

♦ I guess it's ok if I'm in the mood for it. *Kayla*

♦ It makes me feel stupid. I don't ask anything and I just shake my head like I understand and say yes I get it. *Emma*

♦ Sometimes I like it . . . sometimes I don't. *Joseph*

The range of their comments cemented what I believe about rigor. It is important for us to challenge our students, but we must do so in a way that ensures their success, rather than reinforcing their negative feelings.

It's Your Turn!

It's Your Turn!

Do you sometimes struggle with the concept of rigor? Does the concept of a tug-of-war reflect how you feel? Which of the students' comments resonated with you?

_____

_____

_____

_____

Where Do I Go from Here?

Let me be clear about my perspective. I support policies that ensure equitable access to high-level classes, such as Advanced Placement or International Baccalaureate courses. I believe that we need to assess what we are doing in our schools and develop plans for school improvement, whether that is incorporating the CCSS, providing professional development that is focused on vertical alignment, or ensuring that our students who are most at risk for failure have a high-quality teacher.

However, I believe that real change, lasting change, change that impacts the students who need it the most, happens at the classroom level. The true power of making a difference for a student lies in the hands of the teacher. The teacher is **always** the key. It's not the textbook, or the latest program on the market, or even a policy. It is how an individual teacher—it is how **you** use the textbook or program with your students. It is how **you** implement the policy. Throughout this book, we will focus on what you can do in your classroom to increase rigor to benefit your students.

In classrooms where all students learn, regardless of gender, ethnicity, poverty level, or background, teachers do two things. First, they care about their students. The old proverb is true: students really don't care how much you know until they know how much you care. Building a strong relationship with your students is important, but it isn't enough. You also have to care enough to connect to your students in ways that help them rise to higher levels.

That is the core of my view of rigor. Rigor is ensuring that each student you teach is provided the opportunity to grow in ways they cannot imagine.

Keep in mind three beliefs that are guideposts for our journey.

Three Foundational Comparisons
- Quality . . . not Quantity
- Everyone . . . not just "Special Students"
- Learning . . . not Punishment

First, we will center our attention on quality, not quantity. As we discussed in Myths of Rigor, rigor is not about increasing the number of homework problems assigned. True rigor does more with less, preferring depth over breadth. Next, rigor is not just for your advanced students. Rigor is for every student you teach. That includes your students who are at risk of failure, your students with special needs, and your students for whom English is not their native language. We will not be able to explore those areas fully in this book, but for now, remember that rigor is for everyone. Finally, the heart of authentic rigor is learning, not punishment. It is about growth and success, not failure. Throughout this book, our focus will be on how you can lead your students to higher levels of rigor in a positive, productive manner through your expectations, through your support, and through your instruction.

Definition of Rigor

Rigor is creating an environment in which each student is expected to learn at high levels, each student is supported so he or she can learn at high levels, and each student demonstrates learning at high levels.

In other words, we are going to focus on things you can do every day to help your students. Together, we'll discuss practical strategies you can incorporate immediately into your classroom. Are you ready?

It's Your Turn!

In chapter 7, Raise Expectations, we're going to talk about using vision letters with your students. However, I'd like you to take a minute to use that strategy to set your own vision for rigor in your classroom or school. Write a letter to a friend or colleague. Project yourself into the future; date it one year from today. Now, explain what happened in your classroom over the last year as you increased rigor. What did you do? How did your students respond over time? What was your biggest success? Even though you are writing what you hope will happen, write it in past tense, as though it has already occurred.

```
Date:
Dear _____ ,




















```

Conclusion

The case for increased rigor is clear. If we want to prepare our students for a future after they leave school, we must provide experiences that are more challenging. However, we need to move forward with a positive approach to help all our students succeed. Our approach to rigor will shine the spotlight on your classroom, providing strategies related to your curriculum, your instruction, and your assessment.

Final Insights

- The most important idea I read was . . .

- One way I plan to apply this information in my classroom is . . .

- I wonder . . .

2

Digging Into Rigor

Rigor is creating an environment in which each student is expected to learn at high levels, each student is supported so he or she can learn at high levels, and each student demonstrates learning at high levels.

In chapter 1, The Case for Rigor, I introduced my definition of rigor: creating an environment in which each student is expected to learn at high levels, each student is supported so he or she can learn at high levels, and each student demonstrates learning at high levels.

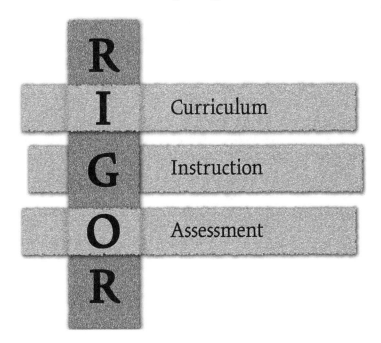

Notice we are looking at the environment you create. Our tri-fold approach to rigor is not limited to the curriculum students are expected to learn. It is more than a specific lesson or instructional strategy. It is deeper than what a student says or does in response to a lesson. True rigor is the result of weaving together the elements of curriculum, instruction, and assessment in a way that maximizes the learning of each student.

Expecting Students to Learn at High Levels

Characteristics of Expecting Students to Learn at High Levels
♦ High Expectations
♦ The Common Core State Standards
♦ Instruction: High-Level Questioning
♦ Instruction: Differentiation and Multiple Intelligences

Let's look at this definition in more detail. First, rigor is *creating an environment in which each student is expected to learn at high levels*. Having high expectations starts with the decision that every student you teach has the potential to be the best, no matter what. There are times this is hard, but I've always remembered that students live up to or down to our level of expectation for them. Expecting every student to learn at high levels begins with the curriculum, or content of your lesson. If you think about Gabrielle's comment from chapter 1, that was her point. We can fall into the trap of reviewing content too much or settling for more basic content. Therefore, we need to evaluate what we teach. One of the main ways we raise our expectations in terms of content is through our standards. Currently, the Common Core State Standards provide a clear set of expectations for increased rigor.

The Common Core State Standards
At the heart of the new Common Core State Standards is a focus on higher expectations. One of the major reasons for a push for the standards was the lack of rigor in many schools today, and the need to better prepare students for college and the workforce.

Developed in a climate of conflicting definitions and perceptions of rigor, the CCSS succeeded in providing a well-defined set of expectations for each grade level in the areas of reading/language arts and math. According to the Fordham Institute's study, *The State of State Standards* (July 2010), the CCSS "are clearer and more rigorous than today's ELA standards in 37 states and today's math standards in 39 states."

The CCSS provide three key benefits:

1. By setting forth a clear and consistent set of expectations for each grade level, the standards provide teachers and parents with what students should know and be able to do at every grade level, K–12. With common outcomes in place, next steps, including the design of curriculum and assessments, can benefit from the collaborative efforts of educators across the country. Additionally, parents and students will know the learning expectations, even if they move to a new school or state.
2. The Common Core State Standards Initiative (www.corestandards.org) was able to develop learning standards informed by the most rigorous and successful models from states across the country as well as from countries around the world.
3. These raised standards are aligned with college and twenty-first-century work expectations. The intent is to ensure that U.S. students will possess competencies that make them successful in the global marketplace.

The CCSS set rigorous benchmarks; however, their impact on student learning depends upon their implementation. True rigor encompasses high expectations for student learning, increased support so students can learn at higher levels, and the ultimate result of rigor—increased learning demonstrated by each student. We cannot assume that simply adopting the standards provides a rigorous environment for students. Rigor is more than what you teach, it's how you teach and how students show you they understand. The CCSS are an excellent foundation for increasing rigor in your classroom; however, there are other integral aspects of rigor to consider.

It's Your Turn!
What are the benefits of the CCSS? What are the limitations?

_____

_____

_____

_____

We also need to evaluate how we ask students to interact with that content, or the way we approach instruction. There are three areas of related research that are foundational to the suggestions provided throughout this book: Levels of Questioning, Differentiated Instruction, and Multiple Intelligences Theory.

Levels of Questioning

Understanding is similar to climbing a mountain. You may have to start at the bottom, but to get the full view (the rigorous view), you have to make it to the top. You climb to the top one step at a time; the steps become increasingly more difficult as you go, but the view is worth it. There are many models for organizing higher levels of questions, but we will look at three. Each takes a slightly different approach, and can be adapted for your precise purposes.

Three Models for Questioning
- New Bloom's Taxonomy
- Ciardello's Four Types of Questions
- Quality QUESTIONS

New Bloom's Taxonomy

The original Bloom's Taxonomy of Educational Objectives, released in 1956, was designed to help teachers write objectives and create tests to address a variety of levels of understanding. In 2001, a group of researchers revised the original taxonomy.

By crossing the knowledge row with the process column, you can plan objectives, activities, and assessments that allow students to learn different types of knowledge using a variety of processes. The revised taxonomy is a complex but useful method for addressing all levels of questioning. Note that numerous verbs in the columns and column headers correspond to key words in the Common Core standards; *analyze, infer, produce,* and *evaluate* are a few examples. This correlation highlights the types of complex thinking that helps students demonstrate learning in a rigorous classroom environment.

Bloom's Taxonomy of Educational Objectives

The Knowledge Dimension	The Cognitive Process Dimension					
	Remember	Understand	Apply	Analyze	Evaluate	Create
Factual	recognize	interpret	execute	organize	critique	construct
Conceptual	recall	classify	employ	disseminate	assess	produce
Procedural	define	summarize	implement	investigate	review	conceptualize
Metacognitive	distinguish	infer	perform	differentiate	judge	generate

Source: Anderson, Lorin W., David R. Krathwohl, *A Taxonomy For Learning, Teaching, And Assessing: A Revision Of Bloom's Taxonomy of Educational Objectives* published by Allyn and Bacon, Boston, MA. Copyright © 2001 by Pearson Education. Adapted by permission of the publisher.

Note: The verbs are interchangeable among the columns. For example, one could *recognize* factual, conceptual, procedural, and/or metacognitive information.

Ciardiello's Four Types of Questions

In *Did You Ask a Good Question Today?* (1998), Angelo V. Ciardiello identified four types of questions, as well as corresponding question stems and cognitive operations. They are simple, but provide a clear framework for crafting questions and assignments.

Ciardiello's Four Types of Questions		
Question Type	*Question Stems*	*Cognitive Operations*
Memory	Who, what, when, where?	Naming, defining, identifying
Convergent Thinking	Why, how, in what ways?	Explaining, comparing, contrasting
Divergent Thinking	Imagine, suppose, predict, if/then, how might?	Predicting, hypothesizing, inferring
Evaluative Thinking	Defend, justify, judge	Valuing, judging, justifying choices

Quality QUESTIONS

When I wrote *Classroom Motivation from A to Z*, I included a chapter on good questioning. I developed nine reminders, around the acrostic of QUESTIONS, to help guide your development of questions during lessons.

Characteristics of Good Questioning

Q—quality
Don't waste your time on questions that are unclear, confusing, or irrelevant.

U—understanding
Make sure your questions lead to an understanding of content.

E—encourage multiple responses
Questions with more than one answer lead to higher levels of thinking.

S—spark new questions
If your question encourages students to ask more questions, you've struck gold!

T—thought-provoking
Prompting students to think is the truest aim of good questions.

I—individualized
Customize questions to your content and to your students.

O—ownership shifted to students
Give students the opportunity to create their own questions.

N—narrow and broad
Some questions are focused, some more open-ended. Use a balance. This is particularly helpful with close reading in the CCSS.

S—success building
Remember the goal of all questioning: successful student learning.

As you create and adapt lessons to incorporate more rigorous opportunities for learning, you will need to consider the questions that are embedded within your instruction. I recently talked with a teacher who was using higher standards and more complex activities, but asked her students basic recall or memory-based questions to assess their understanding. That defeats your purpose. Higher-level questioning, such as the the text-based and inferential questions required by the Common Core State Standards in Reading, is an integral part of a rigorous classroom.

It's Your Turn!

How do you currently develop questions to use during your instruction? Which of the three models described would help you improve your questioning skills?

_____

_____

_____

_____

_____

_____

_____

_____

_____

Differentiated Instruction and Multiple Intelligences

Differentiated Instruction (DI) is a popular concept, and I hear many interpretations of its meaning. For most teachers, it means creating lessons that include different elements to meet the needs of each individual student in a diverse classroom. According to the technical definition, in DI, a teacher varies the content (what), process (how), or product (demonstration of learning) of instruction to enhance student understanding.

One concern I hear from teachers is that differentiation means some students will miss some aspects of learning. In sports, there are basic warm-up exercises and drills for every player on the team. Good coaches also work with each player during practice to increase strengths and strengthen any weaknesses. During instruction, we need to do the same thing. We should teach core information to everyone, and adjust our lessons based on what we know about our students to help every individual reach his or her potential.

One of the ways you can differentiate instruction is through the use of Howard Gardner's Multiple Intelligences Theory. In *Frames of Mind: The Theory of Multiple Intelligences* (1983), he proposed eight intelligences, or ways people learn most effectively.

Gardner's Multiple Intelligences	
Intelligence	*Learns Best Through . . .*
Linguistic	Words/language
Logical-Mathematical	Logic and/or numbers
Spatial	Visuals or pictures
Musical	Rhythms and/or music
Intrapersonal	Self-reflection and/or individually
Bodily-Kinesthetic	Physical activity
Interpersonal	Social interaction
Naturalist	Experiences in nature

Once you understand the different intelligences, you can use them to create activities that will enhance learning for your students. I met with a teacher who told me that this means that you should find out each student's type of intelligence, and then only teach him/her lessons in a way that matches that intelligence. I find that to be limiting, and unrealistic for today's classrooms. Instead, incorporating activities that address various intelligences allows students to construct deeper knowledge by seeing the concept through the different intelligence lenses. For example, I may be a linguistic learner, but my knowledge of geography is certainly enhanced through visuals (spatial). So, although you may want to provide instruction individually tailored to a student's intelligence(s), also plan lessons for all students that incorporate elements of the different intelligences. The Common Core standards' inclusion of visual, audio, and digital texts in addition to print texts, and its emphasis on collaboration with peers in small and larger groups are natural opportunities to address multiple intelligences.

A final important note about differentiated instruction and multiple intelligences: you don't have to incorporate activities for all intelligences. That is likely not practical on a regular basis. However, you will see in the upcoming chapters that there are ways to incorporate the intelligences into your existing lessons.

It's Your Turn!

Are you familiar with Differentiated Instruction and Multiple Intelligences Theory? If so, how do you anticipate this will assist you in your efforts to increase rigor? If not, what is your initial response to this new information?

_____

_____

_____

Supporting Each Student to Learn at High Levels

> ### *Characteristics of Supporting Each Student to Learn at High Levels*
> ◆ Addressing Motivation (Value and Success)
> ◆ Increasing Student Engagement

The instructional strategies we choose directly impact the second part of our definition: *each student is supported so he or she can learn at high levels*. It is critical that we craft lessons that move students to more challenging work while simultaneously providing ongoing scaffolding to support them as they learn. We simply cannot increase our expectations without helping students learn to move with us to those higher levels. Rigorous lessons incorporate elements of motivation and engagement in order to help students succeed. In the most effective classrooms, all three elements are linked together.

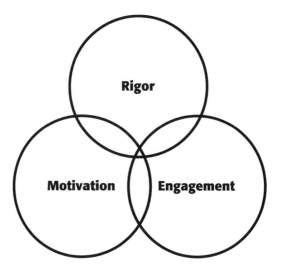

Student Motivation

If you've read *Classroom Motivation from A to Z*, you know that I believe all students are motivated, just not necessarily by the things we would like. Many of my students were not motivated by a desire to learn; rather, they were motivated by the approval of their friends, or the wish to earn some money, or something else in their lives. In our school, we had a basic system of positive and negative consequences, but it seemed to yield temporary results. I used praise and rewards in my classroom, but with less emphasis. I learned that it was more important for my students to be intrinsically motivated, and that my job was to create an environment in which they were more likely to be motivated.

People are more motivated when they value what they are doing and when they believe they have a chance for success. Those are the two keys: value and success. Do students see value in your lesson? Do they believe they can be successful?

Value

There are many recommendations relating rigor to relevance. That is the value part of motivation. Students are more motivated to learn when they see value, or the relevance of learning. I've found that students have a radio station playing in their heads: WII-FM—*What's In It For Me*? When I'm teaching, students are processing through that filter. What's in this lesson for me? Why do I need to learn this? Will I ever use this again?

Ideally, your students will make their own connections about the relevance of content, and you should provide them opportunities to make those connections independently. But there are also times that you will need to facilitate that understanding. I observed a science teacher who was very effective in helping his students see value in lessons. At the beginning of the year, he asked his students to write about their goals for life after high school. During a lesson on chemical mixtures, he realized that Shaquandra was tuning him out. He asked her, "Why is an understanding of chemical mixtures important to you?" Puzzled, she replied, "I don't know. I don't think it is." He then guided her to a realization that, since she wanted to own a beauty shop, she would need to know about mixtures when using chemical treatments on a customer's hair. Her motivation to participate in the lesson increased tremendously. We'll discuss several ways you can tap into your students' goals and dreams in chapter 7, Raise Expectations.

When I lead workshops on motivation, teachers work together in subject area groups to identify the value of a lesson, looking at it from the perspective of their students. Recently, a middle school math teacher told me her students didn't see value in a lesson. One student commented, "We are only doing this because it's on the test." There are times that we teach something to prepare students for a test, but that answer does not typically enhance a student's appreciation of the relevance. The teacher was confused, since the lesson was on positive and negative integers, a concept with many practical applications. Before she could respond, another student chimed in. "Half our football team is in this class, and we're playing Thursday night. Think of the football field as a number line. Positive and negative integers are yards gained and lost." The math teacher told me how much she appreciated the comments from the students. As she pointed out, "It was a good reminder for me. Sometimes, I focus so much on the content; I forget to think about it like the students do." That's the view we need to consider. Through that process, we'll help our students see value in our lessons.

It's Your Turn!

Look at two or three lessons or units you will be teaching in the near future. What is the value or relevance, from the perspective of your students?

Showing Value in Lessons	
Lesson or Unit	What's In It For Your Students?

Success

Success is the second key to student motivation. Students need to achieve in order to build a sense of confidence, which is the foundation for a willingness to try something else. That in turn begins a cycle that results in higher levels of success, both in academic performance and collage and career readiness. Success leads to success, and the achievements of small goals or tasks are building blocks to larger ones.

Success Cycle

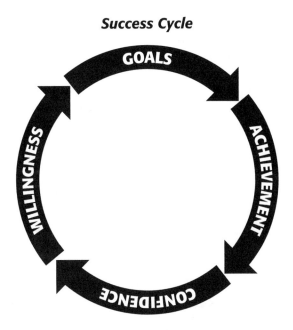

In chapters 3 to 7, we'll look at ways to increase rigor in your classroom. Each recommended strategy is designed to ensure your students' success. However, chapter 5, Give Appropriate Support and Guidance will focus specifically on strategies to support their new learning, and to scaffold growth to increased levels for every student.

Don't underestimate the importance of this motivational element. There are two related misconceptions that are stumbling blocks on the road to rigor.

Misconceptions
♦ Students can't do harder work.
♦ Students do not like hard work.

First, we say that some students can't do harder work. I can assure you of one thing: if you don't believe in your students, they will go out of their way to prove you right. In chapter 7, Raise Expectations, we'll look at how to adjust our perspective of their success. For now, it's important to realize that if you believe your students will fail, they know it, and they believe you. And if students don't believe they can be successful, many will give up before they begin.

Next, we assume that students do not like hard work. Very few students will come to you begging for more work. Some of that is a defense mechanism: "Wait a minute, harder? More challenging? What if I can't?" For others, they'll say one thing to you when their friends are around; but they would have a completely different answer if no one else is listening.

I have served as a team leader for the Southern Regional Education Board (SREB). Schools invite a team to come to their middle or high school to provide feedback for school improvement. I particularly enjoy interviewing students. You discover information from them that you simply wouldn't get otherwise. One of the questions is: "Quality learning is the result of considerable effort to do something exceedingly well. Give an example of an experience that required you to work hard and in which you did well." The answer I have heard most often is a special project, such as something they did for the science fair. Just about every time, they struggle to even think of an answer.

Actually, students associate feelings of success and satisfaction with challenging work when it is accompanied by appropriate support. They also believe that hard work is important. Students are very insightful; if you give them busy work, they immediately recognize it for what it is. But if you engage them in authentic, real-life problem solving at high levels of challenge (think of skills and tasks required by the CCSS, for example), they know you believe in them and respect them. In turn, they will respond appropriately.

It's Your Turn!

Think of your current students. Make a list of those who are successful in your class, and those who aren't. For those who aren't, how can you help them achieve success in your class?

Levels of Student Success	
Successful Students	*Students Who Are Not Successful*

Thoughts for my consideration:
Why are some of these students less successful?

Am I possibly sending messages that I don't believe in them?

What else do I need to think about related to this as I continue reading this book?

Student Engagement

What exactly is student engagement? I read a comment from a teacher on an Internet bulletin board. He said that his students seemed to be bored, and after talking with them, he realized that they were tired of just sitting and listening. He said they wanted to be more involved in their learning. I was excited to read further as the teacher said he decided then to "change how I teach, so now I make sure I do one activity each month with my class." How sad. That means 19 days per month of no activity. That's the perfect picture of what student engagement is not. Don't misunderstand me. There is a place in teaching and learning for lecture/explanations and teacher-led discussions. But somehow, many teachers fall into the trap of believing that lecturing AT or explaining TO works. Perhaps it comes from our own experience. Many of my teachers taught that way—it's what we saw most of the time. But how many of those teachers were really outstanding? Not many. My best, most memorable teachers were highly engaging. I felt as though we were learning together.

I also remember that, as I grew older, the more I was talked at. When did we somehow decide that as children grow up, they should be less involved in their own learning? Let's be clear on some foundational points:

1. Although students can be engaged in reading, reading the textbook (or the worksheet) and answering questions is not necessarily engaging.
2. Although students can be engaged in listening, most of what happens during a lecture isn't engagement.
3. Although students working together in small groups can be engaging, simply placing them in groups to read silently and answer a question isn't. When one or two students in a group do all the work, that isn't engagement. Small groups don't guarantee engagement just like large groups don't automatically mean disengagement.

What does it mean to be engaged in learning? In brief, it boils down to what degree students are involved in and participating in the learning process. If I'm actively listening to a discussion, possibly writing down things to help me remember key points, I'm engaged. But if I'm really thinking about the latest video game while nodding so you think I'm paying attention, then I'm not. It really is that simple. Of course, the complexity is dealing with it.

Think for a moment about a slinky. For a slinky to work, you have to use two hands to make it go back and forth. If you hold it in one hand, it just sits there, doing nothing. It doesn't move correctly without both ends working. Similarly, if the teacher is the only one involved in the lesson, then it isn't as effective. The foundation of instructional engagement is involvement by both the teacher and the student.

It's Your Turn!

Reflect on a lesson you taught recently. Use the guiding questions to think about the level of student engagement.

Lesson Reflection About Student Engagement	
Type of Activity	*Percentage of Lesson*
Teacher Lecture/Teacher Talk During Discussion	
Individual Students' Responses During Lecture/Discussion	
Students Talking to Each Other (Partners, Small Groups)	
Students Involved in Written Response to Learning (Individual)	
Students Involved in Project or Creative Response to Learning (Individual, Partner, Small Groups)	
Other:	
How can I adjust this lesson to increase student engagement?	

Rigor Does Not Stand Alone

In order to effectively increase the rigor in your classroom, it is essential to incorporate elements of student motivation and engagement. In *The Silent Epidemic* (2006), 47% of the high school dropouts who participated in the study stated that one of the major reasons they quit school was that their classes were not interesting. As a result, they were disengaged. There is a clear link between motivation and engagement, and when you increase expectations without considering those two factors your students are more likely to fail. If we want to help all our students succeed at high levels, we must tap into their intrinsic motivation by helping them see value in our lessons, provide support for them to be successful, and structure our lessons to ensure high levels of engagement. By doing so, students will respond more positively to the increased expectations. Then their learning will increase.

Demonstrating Learning at High Levels

Characteristics of Demonstrating Learning at High Levels
- ◆ Challenging Assessments
- ◆ Varied Assessments
- ◆ Formative Assessments

Finally, in a rigorous classroom, *each student demonstrates learning at high levels.* You might think, "If I provide more challenging lessons that include extra support, won't this last part just happen?" I wish teaching were that easy. Nothing "just happens." If we want students to show us they understand what they learned at a high level, we also need to design assessments that provide them the opportunity to demonstrate they have truly mastered new content. Throughout the upcoming chapters, you will notice that many of the learning activities are, in themselves, an assessment of student understanding. As I said earlier, it is critical to incorporate higher-level questioning throughout the process, or you will dilute the quality of learning.

You may choose to use a test to check for mastery of content, but we'll be looking at other alternatives to move beyond testing. Varying the types of assessments you use will produce quality, sometimes from unexpected sources.

For example, Scott Bauserman, from Decatur Central High School in Indiana, asks his students to choose a topic from a completed social studies unit and design a game to show what they have learned. The finished product must teach about the topic, use appropriate vocabulary and processes, and be fun to play. As he explains,

> Students had to construct the game, the box, provide pieces and a board, and write the rules. I received a wide variety. One game I will always remember was about how a bill gets passed into law. We spent time [in class] talking about all the points where a bill in Congress or the state General Assembly could be killed, pigeon-holed,

or defeated. The student took a box the size of a cereal box, set up a pathway with appropriate steps along the way, constructed question/answer cards, and found an array of tokens for game pieces. If a player answered a question correctly, he or she would roll the dice and move along the path to passage. But the student had cut trap doors at the points where a bill could be killed, and if a player landed on a trap door/bill-stopper, the player to the right could pull a string, making that player's token disappear from the board. The player would have to start over. Not a bad game from a student who has fetal alcohol syndrome and is still struggling to pass his classes.

Finally, it is important to balance evaluation of learning with formative assessment. We will devote chapter 8, Assessment and Grading to that topic. For now, simply keep in mind that the best assessments help you understand what your students know and don't know, so that you can adjust your instruction to help them learn more effectively.

It's Your Turn!

How does this definition of rigor compare with what you have heard about rigor or read in other books? As you consider the three foundational components of rigor, which would you like to focus on as you increase the level of rigor in your classroom?

Rigor is creating an environment in which:	*My thoughts*
Each student is expected to learn at high levels.	
Each student is supported so he or she can learn at high levels.	
Each student demonstrates learning at high levels.	

Conclusion

Now, let's make this practical. In chapters 3 through 7, we'll look at five specific ways to increase rigor in your classroom.

The chapters follow a consistent format. After a short introduction, we will discuss five useful strategies you can apply in your classroom. In addition to a description of the strategy, you will find examples from a range of subject areas, which can be adapted to your specific grade level and/or content. You may find that you are already using some of the activities. I purposely included many commonly used ones, adapting them to make them more rigorous. I believe that rigor does not necessarily mean throwing away everything you are doing. Rigor in many cases means adjusting what you do to increase your expectations and the learning of your students.

Finally, chapters 3 through 7 are not sequential. You may prefer to start with chapter 5, Give Appropriate Support and Guidance. Or, you may want to read chapter 4, Increase Complexity and then skip to chapter 6, Open Your Focus, because they are similar. That is entirely up to you. On p. 33, you'll find a listing of the topics for each of those five chapters. You can use that to determine where to go next!

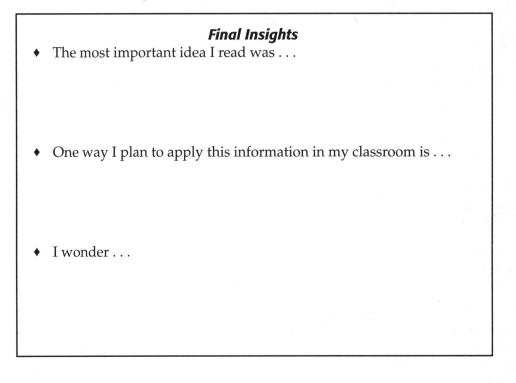

Final Insights

♦ The most important idea I read was . . .

♦ One way I plan to apply this information in my classroom is . . .

♦ I wonder . . .

Overview of Chapters 3 Through 7

Chapter 3: Raise the Level of Content
- Valuing Depth
- Increasing Text Difficulty
- Creating Connections
- Reviewing, Not Repeating
- Planning for Implementation of High Standards

Chapter 4: Increase Complexity
- Complexity Through Problem-Based Learning
- Complexity in Writing
- Complexity as You Assess Prior Knowledge
- Complexity With Vocabulary
- Complexity in Review Games

Chapter 5: Give Appropriate Support and Guidance
- Scaffolding During Reading Activities
- Modeling Expected Instructional Behaviors
- Providing Clear Expectations
- Presenting Multiple Opportunities to Learn
- Working With Students With Special Needs

Chapter 6: Open Your Focus
- Open-Ended Questioning
- Open-Ended Research
- Open-Ended Vocabulary Instruction
- Open-Ended Projects
- Open-Ended Choices for Students

Chapter 7: Raise Expectations
- Expecting the Best
- Expanding the Vision
- Ownership of Learning
- Tracking Progress
- Creating a Culture

3

Raise the Level of Content

The first way to enhance rigor in your classroom is to raise the level of the content you teach. As we have already discussed, many of our students perceive our instruction as too easy. In *The Silent Epidemic*, 66% of the dropouts said they would have worked harder if expectations were higher. As Gabrielle shared in chapter 1, The Case for Rigor, many students perceive lower-level classes as simply "teaching nothing over and over again." However, I don't believe students must move to a higher-level class to gain more understanding. A truly rigorous classroom challenges all students with new content, despite any label. We'll look at five strategies that can help you raise the level of content in your class.

♦ Valuing Depth
♦ Increasing Text Difficulty
♦ Creating Connections
♦ Reviewing, Not Repeating
♦ Planning for Implementation of High Standards

Valuing Depth

In our culture, we are often bombarded with the message that more is better. We can find ourselves so focused on covering material that we only skim the surface; therefore, our students often log information in their short-term memory rather than truly learning and applying it in the future.

When it comes to rigor, less is more. If we expect students to learn at a high level, we must focus on depth of understanding, not breadth of coverage.

I worked with a school district that encouraged summer reading. High school students read one book over the summer and then gave a brief summary of the book during the first week of school. As you might imagine, the quality of the presentations varied tremendously. Some students were creative and provided great detail about their books, while others stated surface information that was available from the Internet.

As an alternative, one teacher required her students to create book webs. In addition to the presentations, each student drew a web connecting their book to their classmates' books. It was their responsibility to talk to each other and discover ways the books were related. In addition to shifting responsibility for learning to the students, the structure of the assignment forced students to move beyond basic, summary information to look for the deeper connections among the various books.

Tonya Woodell points out that rigor is applicable in all subjects. "As a beginning band teacher, the music standards would allow my students to play all grade 1 pieces. The grading scale of music is set from 1–6. Grade 6 music is generally played by very good high school bands and colleges. Although I could allow my students to play only grade 1 music, I expect them to be able to play grade 2 and 3 pieces. And they are able to do it! In Choir, I could allow them to simply sing 'crowd pleasing' songs. However, I expect my students to sing at least one foreign language piece a semester. I also expect that they sing in three-part harmony when unison or two-part would be acceptable."

Another way to value depth is through your vocabulary instruction. My students were often overwhelmed with content-specific vocabulary. The traditional model of vocabulary instruction promotes memorization for a test, but doesn't encourage a true understanding of concepts. We'll look at instructional strategies for vocabulary in chapters 5 and 7, but there is a foundational concept related to depth. Choose your words carefully! In other words, rather than expecting students to learn 10 to 20 words each week, take time to teach critical concepts. In *Building Academic Vocabulary* (2005), Robert Marzano states that of the wealth of vocabulary terms embedded for each subject, some are critically important, some are useful but not critical, and others are interesting but not very useful. That is a helpful way to consider your vocabulary. Prioritize the terms and/or concepts that are critical for students to comprehend your content.

Vocabulary Terms and/or Concepts		
Critical	Useful But Not Critical	Interesting But Not Very Useful

The same concept is true with your standards. You likely have a wide range of standards you are expected to teach. In his newest book, *Rigorous Curriculum Design*, Larry Ainsworth provides a comparison of the Common Core State Standards with older standards and concludes there is still a need for prioritization. He provides six criteria to consider:

- Endurance—Will this standard or indicator provide students knowledge and skills that will endure throughout a student's academic career and professional life?
- Leverage—Will this standard provide knowledge and skills that will be of value in multiple disciplines?
- Readiness for the next level of learning—Will this standard provide students with essential knowledge and skills that are necessary for success in the next grade level?
- School—what students need to know and be able to do at each level of learning.
- Life—what students will need to know and be able to do to be successful after the end of school.
- Tests—concepts and skills that are most heavily represented on external, high-stakes assessments. (Ainsworth, pp. 53–54)

This does not mean that you ignore aspects of the Common Core State Standards. Rather, you spend the most time on the standards from which you gain the most results.

As a final suggestion, take your standards and turn them into questions. What one question would you want each student to answer if they learned what they needed to from your lesson? In other words, if you move past the educational language and extra information, what is the one core thing your students should be able to know or do? What is your focus question?

It's Your Turn!

Do you sometimes feel like you are just trying to cover information? How would you like to shift to valuing depth?

Strategy	My Application
Creating In-depth Activity	
Identifying Critical Vocabulary	
Utilizing Power Standards	
Incorporating Focus Questions	

Increasing Text Difficulty

One of the major areas for increasing the difficulty level of content is through the text used during teaching. Often, we use books or other materials that are not challenging for students. It seems there are two extremes: Some students only read books that are too easy for them; others struggle with text that is too difficult. It's important for students to read a book or an article they can quickly and easily read; those opportunities build self-confidence, provide enjoyable experiences, and may increase student motivation. But if that's all students read, they never learn how to deal with more challenging materials. Reading appropriately challenging material across all subject areas is also a focus of the CCSS.

Particularly at the upper grades, where we focus on reading to learn, we must help our students become independent learners who can capably handle our complex and changing world. A critical part of that process is teaching students to read and understand increasingly complex materials. This premise is in line with the Common Core's interdisciplinary focus on extensive reading of rich texts that build a foundation of knowledge across subject areas.

To increase rigor related to text selection, it is valuable first to simply look at whether or not your students are reading texts that challenge them. You're looking for a balance: Material should be difficult enough that students are learning something new, but not so hard that they give up. If you like to play basketball, you'll improve if you play against someone who is better than you. But, if you play against the most talented NBA star, you'll learn less because you are overwhelmed by his advanced skill level. A good bench-mark guideline is that for text to be appropriately challenging for growth, students should be able to understand about 75% of what they are reading. That percentage means students understand the majority of the material, while learning something new. One option for increasing text difficulty is to identify where your students are reading, and provide text materials that match their level for growth.

As we look at how to incorporate this in your class, let me caution you. Looking at text difficulty should never be a limiting factor for your students. I visited one school where students were never allowed to choose something to read unless it was "within their point range." That is not what I am recom-mending. Students always need the opportunity to read texts of their choice. And there are some books that may have a lower score on a readability scale, but the content is more difficult, perhaps due to the concepts described or due to the use of figurative language. However, I am saying that students also need selected opportunities to read material that is appropriately rig-orous. Please note the word materials. Particularly with students who are reading substantially above or below their age or grade level, consider infor-mational, nonfiction articles rather than novels. This helps address issues other than just the text difficulty. Remember, we are talking about depth, not length, and we don't want students to feel like they are being punished.

When I was teaching, I used books that were labeled on grade level, but in reality, they were much easier than what students were expected to read on the state test or in real-life materials. That is often true today, and that is why it is important to use a measure that is consistent across all texts, includ-ing standardized tests. No matter which tool you use to determine the dif-ficulty of your text materials, it's important to remember that text difficulty is only one factor to consider when selecting text for or with your students. Other considerations include the appropriateness of the text for students' age or developmental levels, the content of the material, and the purpose for reading, such as interest or for research.

It is critical to remember to use your own judgment along with varying measures of text difficulty. However, just because a text is recommended at a certain level does not mean that text is the most appropriate one for your students.

Considerations for Text Selection

♦ Is the content of the text pertinent to my standards or objectives?

♦ Is the content of the text appropriate to the purpose of the assignment (independent reading, research, partner reading, etc.)?

♦ Is the content of the text appropriate to the age or developmental level of my students?

♦ Is the content of the text appropriately challenging for growth (not too hard, yet not too easy)?

♦ Is this the only opportunity my students will be given to read, or are they allowed choices at other times?

One tool for selecting text materials is used in the CCSS: the Lexile Framework. It defines a reader's ability in relation to the difficulty of text. In other words, it allows you to understand a reader's performance, whether on a standardized test or informal assessment through examples of text materials, such as books, newspapers, or magazines the reader can understand, rather than through a number such as a percentile. Used along with your professional judgment, the Lexile Framework provides a way to level books along a "reading thermometer" in a way that is proportional to the standardized test used (see p. 41).

Notice I said, "used along with your professional judgment." Any readability formula should be the starting point for book selection, but it should never be the only factor considered. Remember to think about all aspects of the book or text and preview materials to ensure they are appropriate for your students.

As an example, if I'm teaching a lesson on tsunamis, I might use the textbook section with the entire class. Next, students read a variety of follow-up articles on tsunamis based on their reading level. You can do this individually, but it's also appropriate to place students in small groups based on their ranges of reading levels. Students then "teach" their articles to the rest of the class. Your culminating whole group discussion of tsunamis will be richer based on the expanded lesson.

Lexile

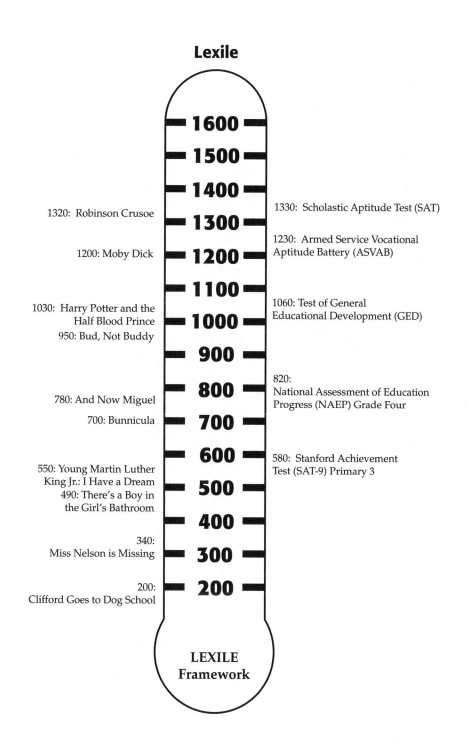

1320: Robinson Crusoe

1330: Scholastic Aptitude Test (SAT)

1230: Armed Service Vocational Aptitude Battery (ASVAB)

1200: Moby Dick

1030: Harry Potter and the Half Blood Prince

1060: Test of General Educational Development (GED)

950: Bud, Not Buddy

820: National Assessment of Education Progress (NAEP) Grade Four

780: And Now Miguel

700: Bunnicula

580: Stanford Achievement Test (SAT-9) Primary 3

550: Young Martin Luther King Jr.: I Have a Dream
490: There's a Boy in the Girl's Bathroom

340: Miss Nelson is Missing

200: Clifford Goes to Dog School

1600 1500 1400 1300 1200 1100 1000 900 800 700 600 500 400 300 200

LEXILE Framework

Another way to customize assignments based on students' reading levels is through limited choice. Rather than allowing students to have total choice as to their selection, require students to choose a book within their reading range. They can still have a choice, but one that is more rigorous. I was sharing this strategy in a recent workshop, and one teacher immediately agreed. She explained that her ninth grader received an A on a report. As a parent, she was frustrated because her daughter simply rewrote a report on *Hatchet* from middle school. The teacher was nonchalant; pointing out that the book was acceptable based on the student's desire to read it. I believe students should have choices. However, if our goal is to improve students' learning, then we must provide parameters of what is acceptable.

A third way to increase text difficulty is to pair texts. A common activity in classrooms is to read a fictional story or novel. To increase the rigor of that activity, add a follow-up activity, comparing the fictional text to nonfiction information. For example, after reading the fictional book *The Watsons Go to Birmingham—1963*, by Christopher Paul Curtis, students can read nonfiction encyclopedia articles and/or magazine articles to compare the story to Birmingham, Alabama, during the Civil Rights period. You could add another step by reading current newspaper and magazine articles to compare it to Birmingham today, detailing the changes that have occurred.

Or, after reading the classic novel *The Sea Wolf*, by Jack London, students can read articles about schooners and the sealing industry. Instead of simply reading and discussing the story, students are required to use research skills, cite sources, and compare and contrast information from a variety of sources. The new activity requires all students to think at higher levels.

It's Your Turn!

Think about one upcoming lesson. Use the grid below to plan a way to incorporate different levels of text materials.

Current information I have about reading levels of my students:
Text materials for the lesson (textbook, articles, etc.):
Strategy to use: _____ Matching students to text through the use of small group articles. _____ Matching students to text through structured choice/book reports. _____ Using paired texts (such as fiction/nonfiction). _____ Other idea I have:
List of other text materials needed for the lesson:

Creating Connections

Another way to increase the level of your content is through interdisciplinary lessons or units. In my experience, this is one of the most powerful ways to help students learn and apply content. It is worth the time and effort it takes for planning and implementation. Begin by choosing a theme, which can be general or based on a particular subject area. Then, pull standards from all other subject areas that can be integrated within the unit. If you teach all subjects, it's easier; but it can also be done by collaborating with other subject area teachers. Either way, you must plan in advance to coordinate lessons and to ensure students have the appropriate prerequisite knowledge in all areas.

Angie Wiggins worked with teachers in other subject areas to create a unit centered on the Renaissance Period.

Sample Renaissance Unit Objectives	
Social Studies	Students demonstrate an understanding of the development and the impact of the Renaissance on Europe and the rest of the world.
Language Arts	Students demonstrate the ability to conduct independent research and use writing to entertain.
Math	Students measure and use a scale.
Science	Students make a model of a working thermometer and collect data on the thermometer. Students collect and organize data to make a scientific inference.
Art	Students create a cityscape using one-point and two-point linear perspective techniques.

To begin the unit, students went on a "gallery crawl" to each classroom. Students viewed pictures and selected works of Shakespeare and Chaucer in the language arts rooms, pictures of Renaissance buildings and toys and games in math classes, pictures of scientists and inventions from the period in the science room, and pictures of works of art in social studies classes. Then, students created word lists based on the viewings, which served as a pre-assessment for the unit.

Students were immersed in the Renaissance period, viewing the time through the lenses of all subject areas. They researched a topic about the Renaissance and incorporated their research in historical fiction stories. Other students created posters about the various professions that existed in the period. The math teachers applied lessons on measurement and scale as students found the perimeter of the Florence Cathedral. In science, after studying Galileo, students created thermometers and recorded data. After studying the art of Leonardo da Vinci, students created perspective drawings. To wrap up the unit, the students celebrated Renaissance Day, which included a display of all student work samples as well as participation in Renaissance games.

After the unit, Angie shared that it was very challenging for the teachers to work together to plan activities that were relevant and appealing. However, the students responded with higher levels of student engagement and overall learning. Throughout the unit, students commented that they were seeing the connections from class to class.

Sample Topics for Interdisciplinary Units

- Tech Training (technology skills careers unit)
- Pi Day (math-based unit around the number pi)
- Greek Mythology (language arts-based unit)
- The Roaring Twenties (social studies-based unit)
- Expressions (math-based unit on shapes and figures)
- Revolutions (social studies-based unit on wars)
- Overcoming Challenges (language arts-based using novels)
- Space and Time (science-based unit)
- Fitness and Health (health and physical education-based unit)

It's Your Turn!

Think about your curriculum. What would be a good topic for an interdisciplinary unit?

General Topic(s) for Possible Unit:	
Applicable Standards for Possible Unit	
Language Arts	
Math	
Science	
Social Studies	
Art and/or Music	
Technology	
Other (Health, Physical Education, Foreign Languages, Family and Consumer Sciences, etc.)	

Possible Activities for Unit	
Language Arts	
Math	
Science	
Social Studies	
Art and/or Music	
Technology	
Other (Health, Physical Education, Foreign Languages, Family and Consumer Sciences, etc.)	

Reviewing, Not Repeating

On one of my school evaluation visits, a young girl stopped me in the hall. After I explained my purpose in the school, she asked if I would tell her teachers something. I agreed, and she said, "Do you think you could tell them that they teach a lot of things we already know? We did most of this last year." Her point, that we often spend too much time reviewing basic content with our students, has merit. I am not suggesting that you stop reviewing content that your students don't understand. However, if a student doesn't know what a fraction is by the time they are in high school, completing pages of practice problems likely won't help.

I struggled with that, too. I had students who simply did not understand basic concepts, so I tried to teach them again. My students still didn't learn it. Repeating the same information over and over doesn't work. A more effective strategy is shifting to a more difficult, authentic purpose for using basic knowledge, and then answering questions to help students complete the assignment. Sometimes, the more rigorous, authentic activity is easier for students, simply because it makes sense to them. For example, I told my students they had to create a classified ad to sell a product of their choice, such as a video game. I gave them envelopes with free words, but if they needed different words, they had to buy them with credits that were included. The word cards contained adjectives, adverbs—everything but nouns. One group tried to write the ad only using free words, and quickly discovered that didn't work. At some point, you have to tell someone what you are selling! It was a great lesson on the purpose of nouns, and was much more effective than the standard review.

When it was evident that my students did not fully understand how to compare and contrast information, I created a folder game. Each group of students was given a folder with a picture from a newspaper or magazine article pasted on the front. The actual article was glued on the inside. Students were directed to look at the picture without opening the folder. Then, individually, each student wrote as many words as possible about the picture, one word per Post-It note. Since they are only writing words, the one-inch by one-inch size of a sticky note is adequate. Next, students talked to each other, using all their words to create a sentence about the picture. Usually, someone asked to add words, such as "the" or "and," or to add punctuation. That gave me a quick teachable moment to discuss grammar and sentence structure. Then I told them they could write anything they needed on more notes.

If you wanted to stop at a basic activity, students could individually write a descriptive paragraph about the picture. For the students who don't know how to begin, they have a group sentence for a starting point. Each group also has a customized word bank of leftover words to use in the paragraph.

However, this activity is more rigorous and can be used across a variety of content areas as we move to the next step. Students open the folder and read the accompanying news article. By comparing their sentences with the actual article, students must use analytical skills. Students use an assessment scale (see chart below) to determine how their work measures up and can revise their sentence if needed.

Scale for Comparing Sentences and Articles
- The sentence is completely reflective of the article and could be included in the story seamlessly.
- Parts of our sentence would fit into the article.
- Were we looking at the same picture?

Sharing their responses incorporates elements of comparison and contrast, and it typically leads to a rich discussion of how a picture does not always tell the full story. This allows me to teach strategic reading and thinking through application, rather than simply telling them they need to be strategic readers. It's important that you choose articles linked to your subject area, in order to help students see the connection of reading with learning your content.

At times, the best help comes from another student rather than the teacher. As teacher Shannon Knowles explains, "I regularly have one student who understands explain the concepts to those who don't. Sometimes, they explain to everyone in class, sometimes to the one or two who need it. They just say it in a way that makes more sense to the students." That is why I incorporate group activities throughout my instruction. By working with partners or small groups, students' learning is enhanced.

It's Your Turn!

Think about your current group of students. Identify several who need a review of basic, prerequisite skills. How will you incorporate review into upcoming lessons for each student?

Possible Review Strategies:
♦ Incorporating review within alternative lesson
♦ Creating review activity with an authentic purpose
♦ Providing opportunities for students to teach each other

Student	Content to Review	Strategy for Review

Planning for Implementation of High Standards

As I've mentioned before, implementing high standards is one of the best ways to increase rigor in your classroom. The Common Core State Standards are designed for this purpose. There are several key steps you can use as you plan for implementation of the standards, such as pulling key words, particularly action verbs, out of the standards. It is also helpful to look at additional descriptors, the appendices, and even the publishers' guidelines to fully understand the intent of each standard. Now let's turn our attention to a planning model for implementation of standards.

When I was working on my PhD, I learned about a planning model from the Dupont Corporation. The Task Cycle focuses on the rationale (purpose) and desired result (product) before determining the process and resources that are needed. Think about how this would look as you plan for implementation of your standards. Too often, we start with the process (how to get there) and resources (what we use) without considering our purpose and the assessment of the end product.

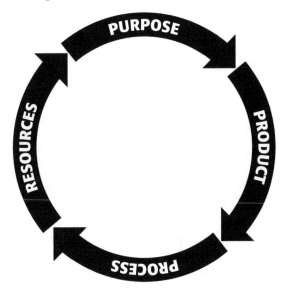

However, with the task cycle, we begin with the purpose: Why do students need to learn this? That can become an important part of our planning and our instruction as we help students see the relevance of the lesson. How does this standard relate to other standards? How does that affect our timeline or groupings of standards?

Next, consider the product—this is how the standard would look if successfully taught. What is the end result? What would good learning look like? In other words, what assessments will you use and how will you know that students have mastered the assessments?

This is similar to backwards design, or "beginning with the end in mind." Planning from the end result—how will students demonstrate learning—is an enormous help as you plan your instruction to match the assessment.

Finally, you plan your instruction as well as the accompanying resources needed to implement the standards.

It takes time to plan using this process. However, if you want to influence your students' learning in ways that go beyond their preparation for the next test, it's imperative to look at the overall picture; to think about your vision, the purposes of your lessons, and ways to help your students grow.

Students who learn to work together to learn are better employees; students who learn independently thrive long after they graduate. And if you want to ensure that your students truly master the standards, then your lessons must support a clearly defined purpose. Be sure you know where you are going, and then design a clear map.

It's Your Turn!

The Task Cycle Plan implementation of a standard using the task cycle.	
Standard:	
Purpose (Why do students need to learn this?)	
Product (What is your assessment? What will successful learning look like?)	
Process (How will you teach this?)	
Resources (What resources do you need?)	

Conclusion

Raising the level of content in your classroom does not mean throwing away your standards or textbook. When we focus on depth, vary our text offerings, create interdisciplinary lessons and projects, and ensure that our content is challenging; even when review is needed, our students will rise to meet our expectations.

Final Insights

♦ The most important idea I read was . . .

♦ One way I plan to apply this information in my classroom is . . .

♦ I wonder . . .

4

Increase Complexity

The second way to enhance rigor in your classroom is to increase the complexity of your assignments. To do so, we need to shift our attention from isolated facts to application of knowledge. We often spend too much time on recitation of facts and figures or repetitious practice. Students need to learn facts, and they need to practice using that information. However, memorization and rote practice do not lead to higher levels of comprehension. Increasing complexity means moving beyond activities that require students to recall information to asking students to apply that knowledge in multifaceted ways. We will look at five specific ways to increase complexity in your instruction.

♦ Complexity Through Problem-Based Learning
♦ Complexity in Writing
♦ Complexity as You Assess Prior Knowledge
♦ Complexity With Vocabulary
♦ Complexity in Review Games

Complexity Through Problem-Based Learning

One way to increase the complexity of your lessons is through problem-based learning. Problem-based learning is

> an inquiry process that resolves questions . . . a problem is any doubt, difficulty, or uncertainty that invites or needs some type of resolution. Student inquiry is very much an integral part of PBL and problem resolution. (John Barrell, p. 3)

What Is the Difference Between Problem-Based and Project-Based Learning?

You may be thinking that PBL sounds a lot like project-based learning, which we'll look at in chapter 6: Open Your Focus. The main difference is that in project–based learning, the teacher directs the questions and assigns the final product. In problem-based learning, the students are more self-directed and come up with many of their own questions.

Although there are various models for posing problems, one that is particularly valuable is the KWHLAQ (Barrel, 1995), which is adapted from the KWL model discussed on page 57 (Olge, 1986) Students, often in small groups, work through all phases of the model to solve a problem.

	KWHLAQ Model
K	What do we think we already KNOW?
W	What do we WANT to find out in order to solve the problem?
H	HOW and where will we find the answer?
L	What do we think we will LEARN? What did we LEARN?
A	How will we APPLY what we learned?
Q	What are our QUESTIONS now that we have finished our inquiry?

Sample Problem-Based Learning Experiences

Kendra Alston, Academic Facilitator at Kennedy Middle School, shared a problem-based learning activity she experienced during a high school social studies class. She wasn't excited to study the 1920s and 1930s, but her teacher, Mr. Baldwin told them he was giving a *show me what you know* final exam. "He didn't care how you showed it, as long as you showed what you know. Things flashed before my eyes, but I was into theatre. So I researched the vaudeville circuit at time and found Bessie Smith in theatre. She was a blues singer who sang in speakeasies; and I learned about the 20s and 30s through her eyes. On day of the exam, I came in singing, staying in character.

He asked questions and I answered based on what Bessie Smith would have said." What a wonderful way to demonstrate understanding of a topic.

I recently visited a kindergarten classroom using PBL. Students were learning about various colors, and one student asked, "are there other colors we don't know about?" The teacher took advantage of this question, and asked students to work with a partner to create their own colors. Students had total flexibility with how they determined their color, how they would explain the color to the class, and how they would show and/or demonstrate the new color. As one student said to me, "it was awesome to answer our own question!"

Darrin Baird used problem-based learning with his marketing students. As he said, "I turned the control to students, rather than me." One day, he brought a box of Cheerios to class. As he discussed marketing ideas for different products, the students began to plan other purposes for Cheerios. They worked in small groups to discover purposes for the cereal, as well as ways to market the product. This open-ended activity enabled students to solve a complex problem of interest to them that was also linked to their class standards.

Sample Problem-Based Learning Starting Points

For language arts, after reading *The Hunger Games*, students create their own societies.

In social studies, students create their own form of government.

In math, students "prove" that math exists with concrete, real-life objects.

In health, convince a jury that asbestos did or did not cause a relative to die.

For science or engineering, design a product that will allow a raw egg to fall without breaking.

Remember, with problem-based learning, there is more control with the students. They generate questions based on a standard or essential question, and then discover the answer through their own research. This doesn't mean that you allow them to stumble through the project on their own; you'll need to guide and facilitate as well as framing parts of the activity to provide a loose structure. As an end result, students choose to demonstrate their understandings in a creative way such as videos, blogs, reports, models, experiments, or metaphors. This learning process aligns seamlessly with the CCSS in Writing that require students to research to build and present knowledge.

Complexity in Writing

Perhaps you would like your students to write a paragraph about the topic you have been teaching in class, such as the solar system. That is a standard, low-level assignment that requires students to restate or summarize the information covered. Even if you ask students to elaborate in greater detail, it's likely that the responses are fairly basic. Instead, let's ratchet up the rigor using the RAFT strategy (Santa, Havens, & Macumber, 1996). RAFT stands for Role/Audience/Format/Topic. Using this strategy, students would assume a role (such as an astronaut in this case) and write from that perspective to a more authentic audience, such as people reading his/her online blog. With a slight shift in the assignment details, students are required to understand the topic at a higher level in order to complete the task. Additionally, when students are asked to write for a genuine purpose and audience, they tend to complete the assignment more effectively. As you can see from the examples, you can tailor this task to your specific needs. For younger students, they can draw rather than write their RAFTs. Also, choose roles and formats that interest them.

Rigor in Writing			
Role	*Audience*	*Format*	*Topic*
Host Ole Winfrey	Television viewing audience	Talk show	Interviewing Aztecs about their culture
Word problem	Student	Directions	How to solve the equation embedded in the problem
Comma	Young authors	Op Ed piece	Misuses of the comma
Water drop	New water drops	Travel guide	Water cycle
Musical note	Composer	Persuasive letter	Usefulness in symphony
Computer programmer	Venture capitalist (funding provider)	Design for new video game	Conflict in the Middle Ages

It's Your Turn!

What specific topics within your subject lend themselves to the RAFT activity? Do you want realistic examples or do you want to be creative and try something a bit more abstract such as the math example given?

Possible Topics			
Role	*Audience*	*Format*	*Topic*

Complexity as You Assess Prior Knowledge

Before you begin teaching a new topic, it's important to find out what your students already know. A common way of assessing students' prior knowledge is through the use of a K-W-L chart.

K-W-L Chart		
K *What I know or* *think I know*	*W* *What I want* *to know*	*L* *What I learned* *(after the lesson)*

Although that can be effective, it is basic, and for some students, it is too open-ended. Pat Vining, a high school math teacher, uses a more complex activity to check students' prior knowledge of a concept and to clear up any misunderstandings the students may have about the topic. First, she gives students three minutes to answer a short true/false questionnaire. Next, in pairs, students compare responses and use the textbook to check their answers. Each set of partners must rewrite any false statements to be true. She ends with a whole class discussion to ensure understanding.

Pythagorean Theorem

Directions: *Note whether the statement is true or false.*

_____ 1. The longest side of a triangle is called the hypotenuse.

_____ 2. In the Pythagorean Theorem the variable c stands for the hypotenuse.

_____ 3. Any side in a right triangle is called a "leg."

_____ 4. A corollary is a statement that can be easily proved using a theorem.

_____ 5. If you know the lengths of all three sides of a right triangle you can use the Pythagorean Theorem to determine if it is a right triangle.

Notice the complexity of this short activity, which is more than a simple pretest. Students must apply what they already know about the topic. Then, they must analyze their responses as they compare answers with their partner, and with the textbook. Finally, they must evaluate the combined information to rewrite any false statements.

Beverly Simon, a fifth grade teacher, gathered very specific data at the start of the year in order to understand her students' math knowledge. Using a chart, she asked students to list what they knew about math and what they wanted to know about math. Then she asked them to work together to create a math alphabet of terms. Through their responses, she learned the broad concepts they knew, then she gained a deeper understanding of their true knowledge based on their existing math vocabulary. An activity like this one, completed in any subject area, helps students to master standards such as the CCSS Language requirement that students acquire and use a range of academic and domain-specific vocabulary.

Missy Miles asks her students to work in small groups to write facts about a particular topic. As a sheet of paper comes around, students write one thing they already know about polynomials, and then pass it to their neighbor. The paper continues around the circle. When it comes around a second time, students can write an additional fact, making sure not to repeat anything another group member has already stated. This continues until the group has completely exhausted all thoughts on the subject. Next, she asks groups to switch papers, read over the other group's list and see if there's anything they can add. As Missy explains, "More than likely they'll see something on the other group's list they hadn't thought of or didn't know." The activity requires students to evaluate for correct content, connect the details listed to other information in their minds, and delete incorrect information, all of which increases the complexity. Collaborative learning activities such as this one are an effective way to include speaking and listening skills, such as those in the CCSS, to content learning.

A final way to help students think about what they already know is by asking them to make predictions. Prior to your instruction on a particular area, give them a list of vocabulary words. I ask my students to work in groups to circle the words they think are related to the upcoming lesson, draw a line through the ones they think won't be related, and put a question mark beside ones they don't know. After the lesson, the students return to the lists to see which ones they predicted correctly. Having a set of words to jump-start the discussion prompted them to think of some ideas that would not have emerged with an open-ended activity such as a K-W-L.

It's Your Turn!

What is an upcoming unit you have planned? Which of the recommended strategies would you like to use to assess prior knowledge?

Assessing Prior Knowledge	
Topic or Unit:	
Correct the Quiz	
Create an Alphabet	
Share Ideas	
Prediction Using Words	

Complexity With Vocabulary

How many of your students struggle with understanding new vocabulary terms? My students did, particularly in social studies. It's difficult to understand the specialized vocabulary found in some content area courses. Words that may seem familiar have a different meaning in the new context. For example, I was in a ninth grade physical science classroom, and Tyler was sure he knew the definition of the term grounded. As he explained that he was grounded for two weeks because of a low grade on a test, the other students laughed. The teacher was looking for an answer about the grounding of electricity, which is quite different. However, it provided an important lesson for the students and for us, reminding us of the ease with which words can be confusing.

When I was a student, the model for teaching vocabulary was simple. The teacher gave the class a list of words. We copied the words and definitions, then wrote a sentence using each term. Finally, we took a test. This model provides routine for students, but it rarely leads to a deep comprehension of the meanings of concepts. Students tend to memorize what they wrote and simply restate it on the test. One of my students just rearranged the words from a textbook definition and said it was her own. In a rigorous classroom, you are looking for your students to demonstrate they understand what a vocabulary word means, usually through an explanation with details, examples, and elaboration. My initial method for pushing students past memorization was requiring students to write an extended response of at least a paragraph explaining the word or concept. However, that backfired on me. My students wrote everything they knew about the topic, hoping I would find the correct portion of the answer and accept it. They equated length with quality while I was looking for depth of understanding.

I learned to create opportunities for students to demonstrate their understanding in ways that required them to synthesize information about a term or concept, and refine it down to the key points. Using a graphic organizer, students discuss different elements of a particular vocabulary term.

Vocabulary Chart

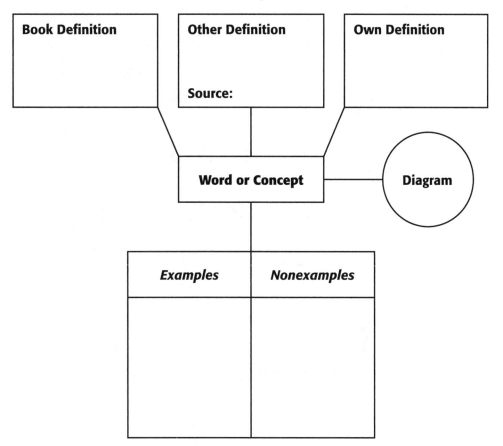

You can customize the headings on the organizer to match your specific subject area. The key to this process is that as students explore multiple definitions, examples and nonexamples, and characteristics or functions, they develop a fuller grasp of the concept.

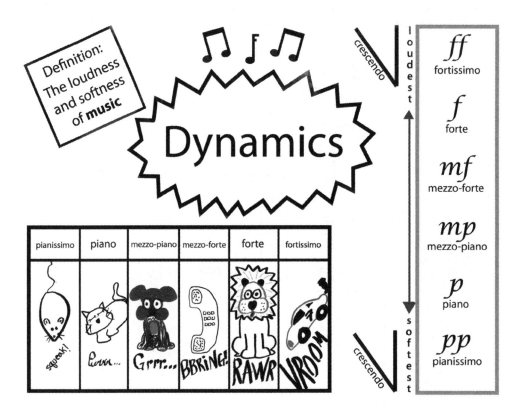

As the culminating activity, rather than writing a definition in their own words, ask students to write a "What Am I?" riddle. When I was at Loris High School, teachers adapted this idea. Their students created "Who Am I?" and "What Am I?" raps to review content.

Sample What Am I? Riddles	
◆ Prices go up. ◆ Your wallet is thinner. ◆ You pay twice as much to provide family dinner. *What am I?* **Inflation**	◆ My end is not like my beginning. ◆ I get bound up for change. ◆ I start low and end up high. *What am I?* **A Butterfly**
◆ Question, question, oh what is it? ◆ Oh, my mind wants to know. ◆ Self-process and problem-solving are a hit. ◆ I'll have to search and find the answer quick. *What am I?* **Inquiry**	◆ I am drawn to scale. ◆ To certain people I am a map. ◆ I am covered with symbols. ◆ Without me, there can be no construction. *What am I?* **A Blueprint**

Elementary students also love the riddles. I was recently in a kindergarten classroom. Students created two-line riddles:

I'm the color of my shirt.
What am I?

I'm what you use when your pencil won't write.
What am I? (pencil sharpener)

The students were excited and worked to make the riddles more complex to "stump" their classmates.

It's Your Turn!

What are several key concepts that are essential for students to understand in your subject? How would you customize the graphic organizer for those concepts?

Design for Vocabulary/Concept Graphic Organizer	
Possible Headings for Graphic Organizer	◆ Book Definition ◆ Other Definition (with source) ◆ Examples/Nonexamples ◆ Characteristics ◆ Functions ◆ Types ◆ Diagram ◆ Elements
Design of Graphic Organizer:	
Sample What Am I? Riddle:	

Complexity in Review Games

Whenever I needed to review content with my students, I used a game to add interest and variety. One popular game is Jeopardy, and my students enjoyed using that format of creating questions to match my answers about a topic. In retrospect, I realize there were times the game was not that rigorous, since some students chose not to participate, except to listen. William McCracken, a science teacher at Loris High School adjusts the process to increase complexity.

I put students into groups with Post-It notes. Then they make up questions from their notes, labs, etc., and assign a point value. Everyone in the group must make a question, and each group must have questions that represent all point values. As they finish a question the students bring the questions written on Post-Its up to the teacher who begins to separate or categorize the questions according to content. The tricky part is making up the category names and trying to come up with something catchy. For example, if I have a group of questions about Boyles' and Charles' Law, I might call the category, "Crime Doesn't Pay" or, "Don't Break the Law." You can have fun with making up the categories, and the students enjoy trying to figure out what I'm talking about.

Notice the intricacy of the process. First, students must create the questions themselves, which requires deeper understanding of the topic. (For more on that process, see chapter 6, Open Your Focus). This also shifts the ownership to students. Next, they must work in their groups to design questions at varying levels of difficulty in order to have questions at each point level. As the game begins, they must analyze the topic headings created by the teacher. Even before you start the actual review, students have been engaged in multiple opportunities to apply their understanding.

Recently, I observed Melanie Auckermann using Jeopardy to review math concepts. In the traditional game, only one student or group asks a question to match the answer. She added a twist, enhancing rigor by requiring everyone to respond. Each group used a small dry-erase board to work through the problems and create the corresponding question. Although she called on one group for a verbal response, every group with the correct answer received points. All students were involved throughout the entire review, rather than becoming distracted or disinterested if someone else had responsibility for the response.

Missy Miles uses a game called "Will the Real Christopher Columbus Please Stand Up" with her social studies students. She explains,

The students stand at their desks, and we go around the room asking them questions about Christopher Columbus or another historical figure we have been studying. If the student gets the question wrong, they must sit down. The level of questions increase in complexity as the game goes on, until there's only one "Christopher Columbus" left standing. The students love reviewing this way. Later in the year, we ask them to create and bring in the questions and answers for the review. Each student writes three to four questions of various levels and puts them in the bank of questions I pull from for the game!

There are many games you can adapt for your students. I used between 10 and 12 different ones, so that students weren't bored. The variety also allowed me to tailor my review toward their needs. For example, Missy's Christopher Columbus game focuses on depth of knowledge about a specific person. Jeopardy is more effective when you have a broad range of information to review. Be creative and involve your students. As we discussed earlier in *Complexity in Projects,* your students can even create their own review games!

It's Your Turn!

How would you like to use Jeopardy as a review game in your classroom? Think through the different ideas as you plan.

Plan for Jeopardy Review Game	
General topic for review	Key concepts to include
Will you determine the categories in advance or will you categorize your students' questions?	
Small group guidelines for creating questions:	
How will you allow students to respond (verbally, on dry-erase boards)? Will you give points for everyone who answers correctly or only the first student who responds with a correct answer?	

Conclusion

Increasing the complexity of your instructional activities is an effective way to incorporate rigor in your classroom. As you consider the examples in this chapter, you probably saw some common characteristics. Each of these examples provides an opportunity for high levels of student engagement, incorporates motivational elements of ownership and value, and demands that students demonstrate understanding at a deeper level.

Final Insights

◆ The most important idea I read was . . .

◆ One way I plan to apply this information in my classroom is . . .

◆ I wonder . . .

5

Give Appropriate Support and Guidance

The third way to enhance rigor in your classroom is to provide appropriate support and guidance to your students. When you raise the expectations in your classroom, you must also provide extra scaffolding for students. Simply expecting them to do more without additional support sets your students up for failure.

♦ Scaffolding During Reading Activities
♦ Modeling Expected Instructional Behaviors
♦ Providing Clear Expectations
♦ Presenting Multiple Opportunities to Learn
♦ Working With Students With Special Needs

Scaffolding During Reading Activities

Since reading is a common activity that occurs in almost every classroom, we will start by looking at several ways to scaffold learning during reading. For many students, a lack of reading skills becomes a stumbling block. The focus of this section is not teaching students how to read. Instead, these suggestions are designed to guide your students through reading so they can understand the content. This section is especially useful in light of the Common Core's inclusion of Standards for Reading not just in the English/language arts classroom, but in history/social studies, science, and technical-subject classrooms as well.

Some students might need your help as they read a section of text. As I heard a speaker say in a workshop, "Don't leave your students alone with their books!" For a struggling learner, reading is like a coded mystery, only he or she feels like they don't know the clues. A Guide-O-Rama allows you to provide clues to the reader. If you've ever written a study guide for your students, this is similar, but with a twist. The Guide-O-Rama intersperses a written think-aloud, so you model your thought processes in the guide. It also takes a conversational, rather than a directive tone. You may choose to use it with selected students or with all students if they are working with a particularly difficult selection. It can be used in class or at home for independent reading. It's important to write questions and comments to encourage higher-level thinking, rather than recall of facts. By incorporating all levels of questions (see chapter 2, Digging Into Rigor) you can craft a guide that allows students to truly interact with the text by making connections, visualizing, creating their own questions, and prioritizing information.

Guide-O-Rama
Europe: War and Change—Chapter 12 (Sections 12.1–12.2)

Page #	Reading Tip
326	Look at the map. This gives you an idea of where Europe is in relation to us. How long do you think it would take to travel there? What would be the quickest way? What would be the most economical way?
327	Read the introduction in the yellow box. Can you believe that most Europeans can speak at least three languages? Can you speak any language other than English? Do you think you need to speak another language? Why or why not?
329-332	Read section 12.1. Pay close attention to the terms nationalism, colonialism, and dual monarchy. They are related, and can be confusing!!! I've found that when I am learning new words that are similar, it's important to write an example along with the definition to help me understand.

(continued)

Page #	Reading Tip
334-338	As you read this section carefully, make a timeline of which countries joined the war and record the dates when each joined. If you like to draw, you might add pictures or symbols to help you remember key events. Do you notice any events that caused a later event? How can you code that so you will remember it? Are there other types of connections that you want to highlight? Is there a different way to visually represent these events?
335	I found it interesting that dogs were used in the war to detect mines and guard ammunition! Do you think this is humane? Why do you think they chose to use dogs this way? Do you have another alternative?
336	Pay close attention to the term fascism. How does this compare to what you know about communism and democracy? Here's another set of words that can be confusing. Because these are broad types of government, I definitely need an example to help me remember them. How can you use what you know about connections to help you better understand related words and concepts?
337	What do you think were the key points from this section of the chapter? What information is missing? Is there a question you still have?

Another approach is an Interactive Reading Guide, which is designed to be used during class. As you can see in the sample on the next page, students work together in pairs to read a section of text. This method is equally effective with fiction or nonfiction. As a teacher, you build structure into the lesson through the guide. I particularly like this approach because it allows me to break the content into smaller chunks for my students. And, similar to the Guide-O-Rama, I am able to direct students' attentions to key aspects of the text. A first grade teacher adapted these activities, and turned them into clues. After creating guides, the teacher cut each step apart. When students completed one step, the teacher checked it and gave them the next clue.

Interactive Reading Guide
Write Time for Kids
"Earth's Baffling Climate Machine"

Individually—Quickly write down your thoughts on Earth's climate. Do you think it's getting warmer? Why or why not? Do you think humans need to change their ways?

Together—Share your thoughts.

Together—Read the expository piece on the Earth's rising climate.

Partner A—Phil Jones makes an interesting statement. When asked about the cause of the warming climate, he says that it is not "a simple case of either-or." What do you think he means by that? Is there another phrase you would use to describe his perspective?

Partner B—Tom Wigley makes a statement about the visibility of rising sea levels. What effect will that have on your everyday life? What will happen if the sea levels rise quickly? Whose lives will be affected the most? How might this affect the creatures of the sea?

Individually—Make connections with what you have just read to information on global warming that the media has put out recently. Use the Internet or newspapers to find updated information.

Together—Discuss what you found. Is the situation getting worse or better? Create a visual that explains your perspective.

Together—Brainstorm ideas on how humanity can attempt to combat global warming.

Individually—Write a letter to the editor of your local paper or write a blog entry about your opinion.

For many students, reading impedes their progress in math, especially when it comes to word problems. There are students who are confident working with practice exercises in math, but who are unable to solve similar equations in the context of a word problem. The graphic organizer on p. 73 helps students break word problems into more manageable chunks. Students look for clue words, such as sum (remember to add), then write what they know from the problem or the given variables. Next, they determine what they are being asked to do, and identify any missing information. Finally, they solve the problem, and write a sentence explaining their answer. The teachers at Chestnut Oaks Middle School who developed the organizer systematically taught their students how to use it and provided multiple opportunities for practice. The picture codes were included to help students easily remember the process.

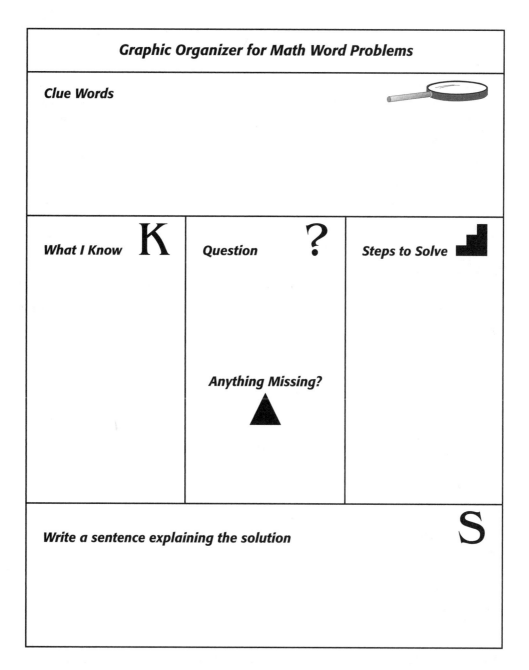

Graphic Organizer for Math Word Problems

Clue Words

What I Know K

Question ?

Steps to Solve

Anything Missing?

Write a sentence explaining the solution S

A final strategy for supporting students who are not reading at grade level is "layering meaning." If a student cannot read the grade-level or assigned text material, find another text on the same topic that is written at an easier level. Students read that selection first, and build their own prior knowledge and vocabulary, then they can go back and read the more complex text with your support. Since the CCSS discourage teachers' building background for students, this is an excellent way for students to take ownership of the process.

It's Your Turn!

Think about your students who struggle with reading in your class. Which of the suggestions would benefit them the most? Determine which strategy you want to use and develop a plan below.

Lesson/Topic for Reading Support:		
Strategy to Use		
Guide-O-Rama ____	*Interactive Reading Guide* ____	*Math Graphic Organizer* ____
My own version:		

Modeling Expected Instructional Behaviors

You likely have some standard expectations for your students related to instruction. However, your students may not understand what to do, even if you tell them. Tracy Smith, a former high school English teacher, found this to be true. "What [my students] really needed from me was a model. So, I sat in a student desk and did what I wanted the students to do. On the first day, it was a little rocky. They came in socializing like normal adolescents. Then, they would notice me and start asking, 'What is she doing?' Someone inevitably would say, 'Oh, she's writing in her journal. That's what we're supposed to do when we come into this class.' Or 'She's reading a book. I think we're supposed to get our books and begin reading.' After a day or two, it became routine."

Another strategy is to model your thinking for students. In other words, you explain to your students what you are thinking. For example, you might say,

Now this year, we're using a new textbook in my class. And one of the things I did was sit down and look through it and see what is available to help me use the textbook most effectively. So for example, you will see a box with words at the beginning of each chapter. Those are important, and they are usually new words, so don't worry if you don't already know what they mean. They are part of the lesson, and there is also a definition in the glossary at the back of the book. I also noticed that in our book, the headings are questions, rather than statements. That's a clue for me—I should look for the answer to the question when I read that section of the chapter.

You can follow the same process with any instruction. The purpose is to show your students how you are processing information.

A final way to model expected instructional behaviors is through the use of standard procedures. One of my challenges as a teacher was content-specific vocabulary. When my students reached a word they didn't know, their first response—in fact, their only strategy for figuring out the new word—was to ask me for the answer. I'm sure that at some time in an earlier grade level, they had learned other strategies, but they didn't use them. This happened so often, I fell into the trap of just telling them the answer, but that certainly isn't rigorous. I learned I was teaching them to rely on me, rather than being independent problem solvers.

I decided to capitalize on what worked in my classroom. I had a set of rules for discipline that they understood and respected; why not try the same thing for vocabulary? So, I developed a set of procedures for what to do when they didn't know a new word. They quickly learned to try other options before they came to me. The most important part of this process was that I made the use of expected, alternate strategies visible and understandable.

What to Do When You Don't Know a Vocabulary Word
1. Try to figure it out on your own.
2. Read the sentence to understand the meaning.
3. Look for prefixes or suffixes that you know to help you understand the word.
4. Check to see if the word is in the glossary or margin of the book.
5. Look it up in the dictionary.
6. Use a thesaurus.
7. Ask three other students for help.
8. If nothing else works, ask the teacher.

You can use this with any instructional behavior. Teach or remind students of effective strategies, keep them visible to everyone, and teach students to be independent. If your students keep an agenda or journal, you might have them keep a log of strategies that have worked for them in the past as a reference.

It's Your Turn!

What are some instructional behaviors you expect from your students? Do all students exhibit them? If not, how will you model what you want?

Expected Instructional Behavior:	
Plan for Modeling	*Plan for Using Procedures*

Providing Clear Expectations

A related issue for many students is that they don't know what "good" looks like. We ask students to complete an assignment, and then we are frustrated when the quality of work does not match our expectations as teachers. This leads us to question whether or not the student cares about doing the work or to wonder if the student tried at all. For many of our most frustrated, and frustrating students, they simply don't know what to do, or how to do it, or they think that they are doing it right!

This often occurs when you ask students to answer questions that require more than just reciting facts, such as describing the causes of an event in history, persuading the reader of a position, or explaining the results of a science experiment. Each of these types of questions requires higher-level thinking skills and applying all those facts they memorized. Some of your students may struggle with these types of questions or assignments. Or, they may be challenged with complex reports or projects. Again, don't assume that it's because they don't want to or just aren't doing it. Many students simply don't know how to do this correctly. As teachers, it is our job to activate or provide background knowledge—not just with content, but with learning processes. First, in order to make performance expectations clear and explicit, we need to discuss the assignment with students.

> One of the tasks you're going to need to complete to be successful in my class is to answer essay questions appropriately. How many of you have written answers to essay questions before? [Students respond] What did you have to do to make a good grade on them? [Students respond, typical answers include: needs to be at least three paragraphs, needs to be at least five sentences, everything needs to be spelled correctly.]

Second, explain your criteria for what makes a good answer, and state these in terms that are understandable to students.

In my experience, teachers generally expect the following:
1. Answer the question. Be on point and don't include information that isn't relevant.
2. Provide supporting details and examples for your statements. *Writing is like a chair; the seat is your statement, and each supporting detail is a leg of the chair. If you only have one leg of the chair, it isn't very stable. In your writing, if you only write one example, the writing isn't as strong.*
3. Have a good introduction and conclusion; start and finish well.
4. Don't make so many writing mistakes with grammar and spelling that I can't read your paper.

Next, discuss the difference between your expectations and their prior experience, clarifying misconceptions. For example, I've found most students equate length with quality, whereas most teachers are looking for depth of understanding, which may or may not be reflected by length. You don't have to tell your students they are wrong; merely explain that you want them to understand what they need to do to be successful in your class.

> You'll notice that my expectations are a little different than what you told me you did last year. Although you can't really answer my questions with just a sentence or two, I don't just count the number of words or sentences. I look at whether you actually answered the question, whether or not you gave at least three examples to support your answer, etc. I know this may be a little different, so let's see what that actually looks like.

Fourth, show a sample answer, either on the board, using a projector, or in a handout, and point out exactly how the sample meets your expectations.

Then, give students another sample answer, preferably on a handout. Pair students and have them read the answer and decide whether or not it follows the guidelines. You might even have them grade it themselves, although I usually start just with satisfactory/not satisfactory rather than A, B, or C. Lead a whole-class discussion, going to each of your points and asking students to explain how the sample compares to each guideline.

If needed, provide a second example to give students an opportunity to practice looking for "good." Explain that, as they write their own answers, they need to do the same things. If students are hung up on a particular misconception, such as always needing three paragraphs, give them a model that does that, but "needs work" in other ways so they can see the difference in criteria.

Finally, move to independent application by giving them a question to answer. Use something simple; your focus in this lesson is on the process of writing a good answer rather than demonstrating they understand new content. Give them a writer's checklist of the guidelines to use as they complete their short essay. During the next lesson, or the next day, review the points with your students through an interactive discussion. As you go through each one, ask them to look at their own essays and check if they followed the standards. Have them physically check each guideline on the paper or the checklist. Then, pair them up again to check one another's papers while you move around the room monitoring their work. Then, give them the chance to rewrite their answers before they turn them in to you for a grade.

Teacher Jessica Chastain uses technology to clarify her expectations for students' participation in their first student-led portfolio assessment conferences. As she explains,

> I taped a sample interview to give the students a good idea of what to expect. When the class viewed the sample interview I would stop the video after each question, have the students repeat each question to me, and then they would write it down. The second time through we watched the whole interview with no interruptions. Then we discussed it. When I interviewed the students throughout the next week, they were prepared to share their work with me, offer me their opinions of their strengths and weaknesses, and we were able to set a goal for the next part of the year.

Since she knew this would be challenging for her students, she showed them a virtual example of the entire process, as well as providing instruction to ensure their success.

For many of your students, they need to understand what is in your head. As one teacher told me, "Most students turn in their best idea of what we are looking for. Sometimes they really don't know what we are thinking, and it's our job to make sure they do know." That defines this strategy; support, engage, and motivate your students to higher levels of learning by making sure they actually understand what they are expected to do.

It's Your Turn!

What is a standard assignment or procedure that is a challenge for some of your students? How will you guide them through your expectations?

Overall Expectation:		
Activating Prior Knowledge	Step One: Discuss their expectations.	
Instruction	Step Two: Clarify your guidelines.	
Clarification	Step Three: Discuss any differences.	
Modeling	Step Four: Show and discuss guidelines using a sample.	
Guided Practice	Step Five: Let students practice assessment with sample(s).	
Independent Practice	Step Six: Ask students to write own sample; self- and peer-assess.	

Presenting Multiple Opportunities to Learn

Finally, there are students who require more than one opportunity to learn your content. This may mean providing additional exposures to learning, or giving them extra time, or creating different ways for them to learn something they are struggling with. As I said to one teacher, providing students with multiple opportunities to learn means moving beyond the old joke that reteaching is saying the same thing again, only slower or louder.

Some students will benefit from multiple exposures to critical skills or experiences. A struggling reader may need the opportunity to experience the text prior to class. In those selected cases, consider allowing students to listen to an audio recording of the material prior to reading it with the entire class. The extra time they spend listening to the text provides a stronger foundation for their comprehension. The Common Core stresses the importance of reading and rereading complex texts, building meaning with each reading. You also might preteach content with selected students, but it's important to find a nonthreatening way to do so.

One day, I tried an alternate method of preteaching with Roberto. He rarely volunteered to answer questions, and generally was nonresponsive in class. Just before lunch, I asked him to stay and talk with me. I explained that on Wednesday, I would be teaching a new lesson, and that I needed his help. We agreed to meet during study hall to go over the lesson together so I could make sure I was doing a good job. Then, I explained that I was particularly concerned about one of the questions I was planning to ask. I said if no one answered it correctly, it would mess up the whole lesson. We went over the answers, and he agreed to help me by raising his hand and responding correctly. Wednesday, Roberto was engaged throughout the lesson, offering answers and asking new questions. That one experience gave him the confidence to participate in later lessons. He also began to read ahead in our book to make sure he was ready for class.

You may have a situation in which a student needs additional time to learn. Typically, that needs to be accompanied by extra support from the teacher. I've been in many schools that provide optional times for students to come in and receive help from a teacher. Unfortunately, some students who need the most help often don't take advantage of the offer. That may be due to an unwillingness to ask for help, or a fear of a negative reaction from peers, but it also may be that it is after school and they don't have transportation. I've also found that for many of our most struggling students, they do not even realize they need help. For a student who isn't mastering your content, don't give him or her an option. Find a time during the regular day when you can provide some individual assistance, and then insist that he or she meet with you. We'll talk more about this in chapter 7, Raise Expectations.

Christy Matkovich points out teachers must find a way to deliver information to students "so their brains learn it. It might be drawing a picture or through movement. If your form of delivery isn't working, then find a different way to deliver it." Ideally, your lesson includes enough options for each student to learn. But if some students don't, then it's up to you to find a new way to help them understand. That's why you've seen activities related to students' multiple intelligences integrated throughout the book. Using that as a part of your framework for planning will help you connect with your students' brains.

It's Your Turn!

Think about your students. Identify three to five who need extra opportunities to learn. How will you help each of them? For each of them, think about whether they need additional exposures to specific content, extra time, or alternative ways to experience learning.

Student	Strategy to Give Him/Her Multiple Opportunities to Learn

Working With Students With Special Needs

Although throughout this book I have provided strategies that will work with all groups of students, including English language learners and students with special needs, I wanted to take time to specifically address students with special needs. One of the most frequently asked questions during my workshops is "How do I work with students with special needs in my classroom?"

Approximately 50% of students receiving special education have learning disabilities, and dyslexia is the most prevalent form. Let's take a look at specific strategies that will make a difference for those students in your classroom.

As Brad Witzel says, first, have high, but realistic expectations for your students. It's easy to lower our expectations because of the label, but that does a disservice to our students. A key concept to understand is that just because a student is labeled does not mean he or she cannot learn. Students with learning disabilities have average to above average intelligence. Therefore, their success in school is not a matter of inability, but of teaching methods and motivation.

Next, consider motivational aspects with your students. We've discussed intrinsic motivation, but with students with learning disabilities, you may need to use extrinsic motivation to help them stay focused on short-term goals. Tokens, check marks, or other outside systems may be helpful.

Third, showcase people who have been successful despite their learning disabilities. This allows students to see beyond their current difficulties to a successful future.

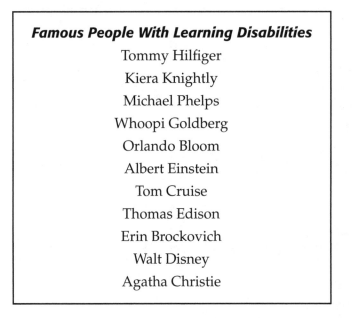

Famous People With Learning Disabilities
Tommy Hilfiger

Kiera Knightly

Michael Phelps

Whoopi Goldberg

Orlando Bloom

Albert Einstein

Tom Cruise

Thomas Edison

Erin Brockovich

Walt Disney

Agatha Christie

Next, use the Concrete-Representational-Abstract (CRA) model to introduce various models for problem solving. "Students are able to choose which method works for them, and then we move on to the next level," says Kawana Dobbins, Special Education Teacher.

Finally, pay attention to the Individualized Education Plan for the student. Does it require modifications, which are changes to what the student is expected to learn? In this case, the standard or concept is changed or is different from general education expectations.

However, some students only require accommodations, which are changes in the way students are instructed and assessed. It's easy to assume that all students need modifications and cannot learn the current standards, but that is not correct.

Possible Modifications	*Possible Accommodations*
Altered grading procedures	Extra wait time
Different reading assignments	Homework reminders and planners
Alternate, but related standards	Visual organizers
Use of calculator during math fluency assignments	Guided notes
	Shortened assignments

Again, many of the strategies throughout the book, especially here in chapter 5, are appropriate for your students with learning disabilities. Simply adapt them to best suit your needs.

It's Your Turn!

What did you learn about working with students with learning disabilities?

_____

_____

_____

_____

_____

_____

_____

Conclusion

As you increase the rigor of your content and assessment, providing appropriate support and guidance to your students throughout your instruction is crucial. The reason I've provided a range of examples is because you'll need them! There is not a "one size fits all" strategy that will support every student you teach. Think about what you already know about your students and their specific needs, and then consider how these strategies can support their learning, recognizing that, over time, you may need to adjust and try new strategies as your students grow.

Final Insights

♦ The most important idea I read was . . .

♦ One way I plan to apply this information in my classroom is . . .

♦ I wonder . . .

6

Open Your Focus

The fourth way to enhance rigor in your classroom is to open your focus. In other words, shift from a narrow, closed focus to a wider, more open-ended one. Rigorous questions and tasks tend to be open-ended, rather than having one simple answer. Many students can complete numerical equations until the equation is embedded in a paragraph that requires them to think about how to use mathematical knowledge to solve the problem. As you create lessons, craft activities that require students to apply what they are learning in a variety of ways. As I've said before, don't ignore instruction on basic facts, but effective instruction always focuses on the use of those facts, not solely on memorization. We will look at five specific ways to open the focus of your instruction.

- ◆ Open-Ended Questioning
- ◆ Open-Ended Research
- ◆ Open-Ended Vocabulary Instruction
- ◆ Open-Ended Projects
- ◆ Open-Ended Choices for Students

Open-Ended Questioning

As you create questions for your students, remember to build in questions that are open-ended that have more than one answer. Although it is important to ask questions about facts and details that have only one answer, higher-level questions generally have several possible responses. The how and why questions will prepare students for life after school. Another way to promote analytical thinking is to follow up on students' responses. Even if a question has a one-word answer, ask your students "How do you know?," "Why did you decide on that answer?," or "What information led you to think that?" By integrating these types of extending questions, you are teaching your students to reflect on their own thinking. Moreover, they gain skill in citing evidence to support interpretations and conclusions, as required by the CCSS.

Another way to promote open-ended questions is through the Question Matrix.

Question Matrix						
What Is	When Is	Where Is	Which Is	Who Is	Why Is	How Is
What Did	When Did	Where Did	Which Did	Who Did	Why Did	How Did
What Can	When Can	Where Can	Which Can	Who Can	Why Can	How Can
What Would	When Would	Where Would	Which Would	Who Would	Why Would	How Would
What Will	When Will	Where Will	Which Will	Who Will	Why Will	How Will
What Might	When Might	Where Might	Which Might	Who Might	Why Might	How Might

Source: Wiederhold (1995).

This grid crosses basic questions (who, what, when, where, why, and how) with verbs (is, did, can, would, will, and might) to create a matrix that addresses all levels of questioning. If you divide the grid into four quadrants, you'll notice the upper left addresses basic questions; and the closer you go to the bottom right, the higher the level of the question. I copy the grid on bright colors of card stock, cut the squares apart, and put a complete set in a plastic bag. After my students have read a portion of text material, or when we are reviewing for a test, I put them in small groups and give each group a bag of cards. In turn, each student draws a card and has to finish the question. For example, if I draw the question card "how would," I might ask, "How would you react if you lived in a country that faced a famine?" Then, the rest of the small group must answer the question. I've done this with hundreds of teachers, and you can use these questions with almost any topic.

I recently visited Dani Sullivan's language arts classroom. She used the Questioning Matrix as a review game for students to discuss four chapters from a novel they read. Her students completed exit slips, responding to the activity. As you see from their comments below, they learned as much about their own learning as they did about the chapters.

Students' Comments About Questioning Matrix

♦ I learned how to quickly think of a question on the spot. I learned that it is also very difficult to come up with questions. I was better at answering them.

♦ I learned that we might have understood the book differently than other people. Meaning, other people might have gotten more out of it than you might have.

♦ I learned if someone didn't read one of the chapters.

♦ By playing the small review game, I learned that even the tiniest of events have a ton of information that can be pulled from it and evaluated.

♦ I just learned that using different words to begin a question greatly affects the answer.

♦ I learned that inferential questions are a lot harder to create and answer than literal ones but no one even tried to make a literal question.

You can also adapt the matrix by creating your own question starters. For example, when I taught a mystery, I wanted to focus on characters, events, foreshadowing, and prediction. So I wrote specific open-ended questioning prompts and put them on cards for the students to use.

Sample Question Starters			
Language Arts	*Math*	*Science*	*Social Studies*
Which character . . . ?	When I compare . . . ?	Which reaction . . . ?	What led to . . . ?
Why did . . . ?	When I order . . . ?	If I did this again would . . . ?	Which events were . . . ?
If . . . ?	What information . . . ?	Why did this . . . ?	How did they . . . ?
Which clues . . . ?	Which phrases . . . ?	How did this . . . ?	Why did they . . . ?
Where did . . . ?	How do I . . . ?	How might the results change if . . . ?	How might things have been different if . . . ?
Which word or phrase . . . ?	I wonder if another solution . . . ?		
What event . . . ?			

Ideally, students could simply create their own questions about a topic. You may teach students who can do that immediately. For example, I spoke with a high school careers and technology teacher. She began lessons with a problem students would face as employees. Her students then created a list of questions that would help them process how to solve the problem. It was exciting to watch them evaluate a problem from many perspectives to come up with possible solutions. However, in my experience, students need a starting point, particularly if they are accustomed to only answering questions from the teacher. The Questioning Matrix is interactive and engaging, but most importantly, it provides scaffolding as you shift the ownership of the activity to students. With regular opportunities, your students will learn to craft high-level questions without prompting from you or the cards.

First-grade teacher Jamie Kistler encouraged her students to create their own questions as they read a short story. Based on a simplified questioning matrix (page 88) they wrote their questions on craft sticks. Students drew a craft stick and had to answer the question. Because they had created the questions, they had more ownership in the game and were more engaged.

It's Your Turn!

How might you use the Question Matrix? Or, would you rather create your own questions?

Lesson/Unit:	
I plan to use the Question Matrix _____ (check for yes) I want to make up my own questions:	
Materials Needed:	Plan for Small Groups:

Open-Ended Research

Several years ago, I heard a speaker discussing the information overload in our information-rich society. He said that the amount of information available to us doubles every 24 hours and that the amount available would only increase in the future. With the Internet, e-mail, and other electronic databases the amount of available information is unbelievable. Learning how to find the information you need when you need it is the purpose of research, not some dry and dull paper on a useless topic.

I told my students that researching a topic was like being a detective. Lindsay Yearta uses the same analogy with her fifth graders. First, she provides a structured Detective Guide for them as they learn the basics of research. Then she guides them through the process, gradually lessening support to enable them to work independently.

Be the Detective!

Detectives always:
1. Get information from a reputable source!
   My information is from:

2. Document all information related to the source. Give credit where credit is due. If you use more than one source, list the others on the back of the guide.

   Title: _____

   Author: _____

   Publisher: _____

   Year published: _____

   Pages that I used: _____

3. Check information twice (Make sure you get the facts straight!).
   ☐   Checked it once
   ☐   Checked it twice

4. Take notes . . . write it down!

5. Put the information in your own words.

Chad Maguire, a math teacher, asks his students to research and write about a famous mathematician. After giving students an overview of the project and sharing brief biographies of mathematicians, he randomly draws students' names, and then they hold a draft similar to a pro sports draft to select their subjects.

The finished report must include standard information about the person, but students also present the information in a creative way, such as role-playing the mathematician or creating a game. As a final incentive, students earn bonus points based on the number of things they have in common with the person they research, which encourages them to move beyond basic information. If you prefer not to use extra credit, simply build this into the standard assignment.

Missy Miles incorporates high levels of engagement for her social studies research activities.

> For biographies, my students dress like their person and give a speech about themselves. When we do colonial research, they write a historical fiction picture book to retell the story of the colony they research. We play "Will the Real Christopher Columbus Please Stand Up" and hold an "Ole Winfrey" show for Spanish conquistadors.

One of my favorite activities with high school students involves research and Wikipedia. Since many students believe that is the only "real" source of information, assign them (or have students choose) a topic of interest. Then, they find 3-5 sources of information on the same topic not used for the Wikipedia article. Students then compare their research with the information in Wikipedia. If they find additions and or corrections, they submit them to Wikipedia. It's an authentic, open-ended activity for students.

It's never too early to begin teaching students how to do research. Connie Forrester describes research projects for younger students:

> I had a menagerie of animals in my kindergarten room (tanks of goldfish and guppies; terrariums with worms, isopods, crickets, and lizards; a resident guinea pig; and an outdoor habitat designed to attract hummingbirds). Since I had arranged the curriculum into integrated units of study, it was simple to study each animal during the course of the year. As a culminating research project, I had the children complete a research project on the animal of their choice. I had 24 children and 8 different animals, so the children worked in groups of 3. Parent volunteers are a must for this project, so go ahead and line them up ahead of time.

Research doesn't have to be difficult or boring. And it definitely should not be something that makes students feel like they are simply spinning their wheels, hoping to stumble on the right information. As teachers, it's our job to prepare them for the future. Research is a key that will help them unlock doors.

It's Your Turn!

How do you already incorporate research in your classroom? What is a new way you can enhance open-ended research with your students?

Open-Ended Vocabulary Instruction

As we discussed in chapter 4, Increase Complexity, the traditional, memorization-based model of vocabulary instruction does not result in long-term learning. However, if you give students a wide range of experiences with words used in context, connect the new information with what your students already know, and provide opportunities for them to play with the words, they will leave your classroom with a deeper understanding of the concepts. The Common Core approach reminds us that vocabulary acquisition best occurs in the context of meaningful learning, not in isolation. In addition to the strategies we looked at in chapter 4, you can also use poetry as an open-ended way to demonstrate students' understanding of vocabulary.

For example, at the end of a lesson or unit, place your students in small groups to create poems about the vocabulary words. I recommend a haiku, the Japanese patterned three-line poem. Line one must include five syllables, line two, seven syllables, and line three, five syllables. It provides an interesting challenge to students to condense the information and present it following the pattern.

Sample Haikus

Atmosphere, it's here
Around the Earth in layers
N, O, H and more

Axis and Allies
Allies were victorious
It's all World War II

Poems have purpose
Express ideas and feelings
Creativity

There was an article in *The New York Times* about a blogger who encourages the use of the Fibonacci sequence to write poems. It is an engaging way to explain math terms, while reinforcing a math concept.

Sample Fibonacci Sequence Poem
Divisibility

1 Math
1 house
2 divide
3 whole numbers
5 remainder zero
8 when the last digit is even
5 Then divide by 2
3 The answer
2 Should be
1 A
1 Whole

Amber, Grade Seven

Another way to make vocabulary more memorable is to have students develop concrete poems to help them remember the meaning of the word. Concrete poetry allows your students to be creative and use visuals. This is more motivating to your students who don't always feel successful with language. Since they must use words that describe or define the term or concept in order to create the picture, it is more challenging than it first appears.

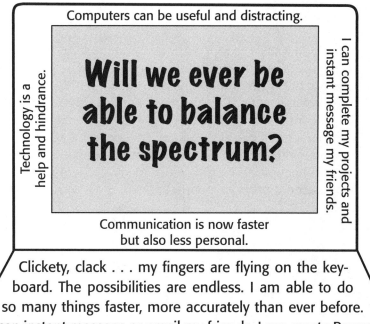

Computers can be useful and distracting.

Will we ever be able to balance the spectrum?

Technology is a help and hindrance.

I can complete my projects and instant message my friends.

Communication is now faster but also less personal.

Clickety, clack . . . my fingers are flying on the keyboard. The possibilities are endless. I am able to do so many things faster, more accurately than ever before. I can instant message or email my friends. I can create Power Points, essays, movies, and songs. I can research any topic that interests me. What in the world did people do without computers?

It's Your Turn!

Think about a future unit or lesson. Pick three to five important vocabulary words. How will you use poetry to help students show they understand the meaning of a term?

Lesson/Unit:	
Vocabulary Word(s)	*Type of Poetry to Use*

Open-Ended Projects

I was recently in a high school math classroom where the students were absorbed in small group discussions of slope and distance. Rather than solving a series of numerical equations for practice, students were asked to design the ideal roller coaster. The complexity and ambiguity challenged students. Students were also motivated by the variety of activities. Each group discussed the characteristics of the desired roller coaster, used computations to make decisions, drafted their design, and built a model. The students also felt a personal connection to the task, since many of them held summer jobs at a nearby amusement park. The varied activities also addressed the multiple intelligences.

Roller Coaster Rigor	
Integration of Varied Activities to Address Multiple Intelligences	
Linguistic	Discussion and writing of plans
Logical-Mathematical	Computation of speed, distance, and slope
Spatial	Drawing plans for model
Musical	Learns best through rhythms and/or music
Intrapersonal	Individual journals for reflection and accountability
Bodily-Kinesthetic	Creation of model
Interpersonal	Group work for project
Lesson Value/Relevance: Some students work at nearby amusement park in the summer. Others regularly go to the park and are interested in roller coasters.	

Missy Miles points out that increasing complexity also shifts ownership to students and increases depth of learning. "As an extension of learning during our Civil War unit, we ask the students to choose the topic they are most interested in. While offering a variety of ways to show knowledge, our intent is to intrigue students and cause them to be constructive learners. The focus is for them to become a class expert at one area of high interest, rather than trying to learn a little about each topic."

Students are given four choices for the culminating project (see table), which incorporate multiple intelligences.

Sample Social Studies Projects	
Musical-Rhythmic: Do you love listening to music? Research Civil War era music. Keep a list of at least ten songs that you have listened to. On the list include the name of the song, the song writer (if known), whether it was Union or Confederate, and a one- to two-sentence description of the mood of the song and what the song is about. After listening to several songs, choose one to research and share with the class. In a typed, one-page report, discuss when and why this song was written. Do you know who wrote the lyrics? Was it a Union or Confederate song? Finally, what is the song about (be detailed and specific)? Why did you choose this song? You need to present your findings to the class (you can simply read your report) along with a copy of the lyrics for the document camera. Last but not least, you'll get to either sing or play the song for your peers (load it onto an mp3 player)!	**Verbal-Linguistic:** Are you dramatic? How about becoming Mr. Abe Lincoln himself? Become an expert at two of his most important addresses/statements to the nation. Read and paraphrase the Emancipation Proclamation and the Gettysburg Address. Your "versions" should be in your very own fifth grade language. Get a copy of the documents from your teacher to see how you should paraphrase it. Then, memorize and perform a dramatic reading of the Gettysburg Address for the class. You could even dress like Abraham Lincoln if you so wished! Your typed, paraphrased Proclamation and Gettysburg Address and your performance will be graded.

(continued)

Visual-Spatial: Are you interested in battle plans and war strategies? Choose a battle from the Civil War. It does not have to be one we have studied in class. Draw a map of the area and use color-coded arrows to show the movement of each side's troops. This should be completed on large construction paper. Pay attention to detail and be able to explain this map and the battle strategy to your classmates. Know important names, dates, and statistics for the battle—you can bullet-point these on note cards or on a visual for your classmates (you could even prepare a few PowerPoint slides to display your facts). You will be graded on quality of facts pertaining to the battle, neatness and accuracy of battle plans (your map), and your ability to explain the battle to your peers.	**Bodily-Kinesthetic:** Would you like to learn about the naval battles that took place during the Civil War? Research the battle of the *Monitor* and the *Merrimack* or the use of submarines during the war. Use cardboard, foil, or other materials to build a model of one of these ironclad vessels. Prepare to share this model and explanation of the ship/submarine and battle with your classmates. Please write your facts and explanations on note cards. The quality of facts on your note cards and your model will be graded.

In chapter 7, Raise Expectations, and in chapter 8, Assessment and Grading, we will talk about the importance of shifting students' attention to learning rather than completely focusing on grades. One key aspect of that is designing clear evaluation rubrics for students. Missy and the other fifth grade teachers also provided rubrics so their students would understand the expectations for the projects.

Rubric for Civil War Song

	Excellent 9-10 points	Average 7-8 points	Weak 5-6 points
Song Analysis	A typed report thoroughly analyzes the song lyrics and provides information about the background of the song. (one page minimum—size 12 font). It is well organized, and spelling/grammar mistakes are minimal.	The report gives basic information about the song but does not thoroughly analyze it (as outlined in the project description). The report may be unorganized and difficult to follow.	The report presents minimal information about the song. No analysis is included (only one paragraph).
Presentation	Your presentation is well-rehearsed. The typed lyrics to the song are provided and shown via the document camera, and the actual song is played/sung for classmates.	You have neglected to provide either the lyrics or the actual song; your presentation would have benefited from more rehearsal.	You have neglected to provide either the lyrics or the song; your presentation was confusing and did not teach your peers anything about Civil War period music.
Civil War Song Chart	An attractive chart with an extensive list of Civil War songs you have listened to is provided along with brief information about the lyrics.	The chart provided is lacking in song quantity, lyric summary, or neatness.	You have not utilized the song chart to help you learn about Civil War music (very few songs and missing summaries).

During a unit on ancient and medieval China, Cheryl Chalmers asked her students to create an advertisement to sell a Chinese invention. Students chose something from Chinese history and researched the good or service. They also applied what they learned about propaganda techniques to create a magazine ad, which included factual information, such as the dynasty or time period of the invention as well as the impact of the invention on people today. The final ads were bound together to create a "Catalogue of Chinese Creations."

There are many ways you can use projects to help your students understand content at a more complex level. Projects can be done in small groups, as long as you provide a structure for accountability for each student, or the products may be completed individually. You'll also notice that by incorporating creative aspects, the motivation of your students is enhanced.

Sample Projects	
Language Arts	"Shakespeare Incarnate": Create and perform a skit as a follow-up to a novel or short story. The skit can be an adaptation, a continuation, or written from a different point of view. Each group has to advertise their play, use costumes that the school owns or create their own, and stick to a time limit. Students then perform the play for peers and/or an audience.
Math	Create objects incorporating Pascal's Triangle or certain shapes (such as a rhombus). As an alternative, create a game that incorporates the use of graphing (such as Battleship).
Science	"Green Plan": Each group must construct a plan to save the environment and live more "green." Language arts skills are also incorporated as students plan speeches to convince the population that living green is the way to go. Students must decide on recycling programs (keeping in mind effectiveness and cost). Students will create charts and graphic organizers showing the efficiency of their plans.

(continued)

Social Studies	"Mr./Madam President": Create a media campaign for the ideal presidential candidate. Each group is a campaign with one candidate, a campaign manager, etc. The candidate must give speeches, have a plan, take a stand on current issues, and win the votes of the population. This is easily adaptable to earlier grade levels, with additional support.
Band	"Music to My Ears": Each person writes their own piece of music, incorporating knowledge gained through their studies. Students can then perform in front of peers in an "American Idol" type of setting.
Career/ Technology	Ask older students to create a Facebook page (www.myfakewall.com) for one of the characters in a novel or short story. Students do an in-depth character sketch in order to have appropriate information for all aspects of the page. Younger students can create a character's culture box, filled with objects, pictures, and quotes, that describe the character.

You might also consider asking students to create their own projects. Think of the ownership and initiative required to design a game. Aaron Arthur, an eighth grader, created a deck of cards to review literary elements such as hyperbole, meter, and external conflict. In addition to the word cards, there were partial definition cards. In turn, students drew and/or traded cards to create complete explanations of the concepts. Another student I met created an electronic treasure hunt about geography. And in one high school I visited, students had designed a video game that required solving quadratic equations to move to higher levels. Give your students the opportunity to be creative and watch them flourish!

It's Your Turn!

Think about your upcoming lessons. Which topic lends itself to a project that requires your students to apply information?

Once you have decided on a project, think about how to incorporate specific activities or requirements that will address at least three of the multiple intelligences. Finally, think about how to incorporate value in the activities to increase your students' motivation.

Planning Template for Incorporating Multiple Intelligences in a Lesson		
Topic/Lesson/Unit:	Project:	
Remember, you don't need to incorporate all intelligences; just use the ones that are most applicable.		
Multiple Intelligence	*Description*	*Component or Activity*
Linguistic	Learns best through words/language	
Logical-Mathematical	Learns best through logic and/or numbers	
Spatial	Learns best through visuals or pictures	
Musical	Learns best through rhythms and/or music	
Intrapersonal	Learns best through self-reflection and/or individually	

Bodily-Kinesthetic	Learns best through physical activity	
Interpersonal	Learns best through social interaction	
Naturalist	Learns best through experiences in nature	
Lesson Value/Relevance:		

Open-Ended Choices for Students

There are many opportunities for students to have choices in your classroom. It's fairly easy to give students choices with a little extra planning. One of the most basic ways is to allow students to choose how they demonstrate understanding of content. For example, when I assigned a report to my students, they could choose how to present it to our class. Imagine the depth of understanding needed for a student to summarize a book in a two-minute commercial or the creativity involved in developing a music video to explain content. If they are allowed to choose how they show you they understand the content, many students will invest more time and effort on the task.

Many teachers use individual learning contracts, which contain a list of activities related to the unit. Students complete a certain number of the tasks for a grade. If you would like a more creative approach, you can turn those choices into a Tic-Tac-Toe grid. Students choose three assignments they prefer.

Tic-Tac-Toe

Interview 3 people outside of Grandview to discover how math is used in their jobs. Develop a set of 5 questions to be used during the interview with a place for signature of the person being interviewed. Present the questionnaire for teacher approval before beginning interviews. If possible, obtain copies of graphs, charts, forms, etc. to illustrate. After the interviews write a summary paragraph of at least 5 sentences. Put all information into booklet with each interview & paragraph on a separate page. Present to class.	Mystery packet of Career/Consumer math problems.	Collect 2 examples of each of the following types of graphs: bar, circle, line and pictographs. (Cannot be from math textbooks.) Organize into a booklet with one graph per page and a paragraph of at least 5 sentences discussing the type of graph, the information in the graph, the usefulness of the graph, who would use the information in the graph and why.
Construct a page of the calendar for any month except February. For each day create a math problem for which the answer to the problem is the date that it represents, its opposite, its reciprocal, or its negative reciprocal. Use as many different types of problems as possible. (Minimum 10)	Design a crossword puzzle using vocabulary terms from the current chapter of study.	Record daily the number of gold, silver & bronze medals won by the United States each day and then create an appropriate graph to display the information. Make the poster as attractive as possible.
Watch TV, read newspapers, magazines, etc. and find a minimum of 5 advertisements that use statistics that are misleading. Describe (from TV) or cut out the advertisement and explain why the statistic is misleading. Display as a booklet or poster.	Research and obtain 2 data sets regarding the Olympics and compare using box & whisker plots. Display both plots on a poster board or on large construction paper. Examples of data sets could be: number of medals awarded to countries of Europe compared to Middle East countries. Or, include a break down of medals won in each event for 2 countries such as the United States and Canada.	In math book complete page 128 (Discovering Algebra). Display all data on a poster making it as attractive as possible. *Thanks to Diane Owens*

You must choose any three assignments Tic-Tac-Toe fashion and complete one assignment each week for the next 3 weeks. The first will be due Feb. 17th, the next on Feb. 24th, and the last will be due on March 3rd. These will be your problems of the week for the next 3 weeks so choose wisely.

I understand that I am to complete 1 project each week for the next 3 weeks.

Signature _____   Date _____

You may consider designing activities for your contracts or Tic-Tac-Toe grids around the multiple intelligences. This helps you ensure a wide variety of options for your students.

Sample Activities for Multiple Intelligences	
Linguistic	*Logical-Mathematical*
♦ Participate in two-character debates ♦ Use dialogue in reading and writing ♦ Play word puzzle games	♦ Create timelines of events ♦ Use Venn diagrams for comparison ♦ Play games to form words using dice with letters
Spatial	*Musical*
♦ Draw or build settings ♦ Create posters ♦ Make 3D projects ♦ Create visual puzzles	♦ Write and sing songs ♦ Associate rhythms with different characters or events ♦ Read and write tongue twisters
Intrapersonal	*Bodily-Kinesthetic*
♦ Keep logs of silent reading ♦ Allow for self-assessment of strengths and challenges ♦ Set personal goals	♦ Role play story or act out words ♦ Impersonate a famous person from history ♦ Create timeline with clay, paint, or sand
Interpersonal	*Naturalist*
♦ Participate in choral reading or Reader's Theatre ♦ Hold mock talk shows ♦ Share writing through the Author's Chair or an Open Mike Night	♦ Go on a nature walk for a prewriting activity ♦ Build a habitat ♦ Identify plants or other aspects of nature

I'm often asked, "Does choice mean I have to let my students do whatever they want?" Notice that in each of these examples, choice was balanced with structure. The activities provide choice within parameters that reflect the adult world. In most situations, you are asked to choose from options, whether it is the purchase of a car, or deciding on a job. When I work with graduate students, I tend to allow more flexibility with their options; but even then, I provide limits. If a graduate student wants to pursue a topic for a project, and it isn't one that I've recommended, I think, *Does It Count?*, using a set of guidelines.

Does It Count

C—Connected to our topic
O—On an appropriate level (not too easy, not too hard)
U—Understandable to you as the teacher
N—Not a repeat of earlier work
T—Thought-provoking

It's Your Turn!

Think about your upcoming lessons. Design a learning contract or a Tic-Tac-Toe learning grid that incorporates a variety of activities.

Topic: _____   Learning Goal: _____

Conclusion

Creating open-ended instruction is really about widening your focus. Rather than providing a narrow range of instruction, you are allowing students to learn in multiple, different ways. In doing so, your students will experience a greater depth of understanding. They will also have better opportunities to demonstrate their learning. Finally, this allows you to provide a more motivating learning environment, because you have shifted the ownership to the students.

Final Insights

- The most important idea I read was . . .

- One way I plan to apply this information in my classroom is . . .

- I wonder . . .

7

Raise Expectations

The final way to enhance rigor in your classroom is to raise expectations. If you think about it, everything we've talked about so far incorporates the notion of higher expectations for students. But now let's look at it from a different perspective. There are five ways to raise expectations.

- ♦ Expecting the Best
- ♦ Expanding the Vision
- ♦ Ownership of Learning
- ♦ Tracking Progress
- ♦ Creating a Culture

Expecting the Best

Just as butterflies are not in their final beautiful state when they are born, or when they are caterpillars, or when they form into a chrysalis, so our students are not in their completed state when we are teaching them.

Think about that for a minute. Where are the students you teach? Are they newborn? Are they caterpillars? Or are they inside a chrysalis? What does that mean to you? If you think about your students as "butterflies-in-the-making," how does that change how you view them? One of the most difficult things for teachers to do is to keep our expectations high, especially when our students' actions make us think less of them. There were days my students challenged me to come up with any positive thoughts about them, but those were the days they needed me the most. I found they needed me to believe they are butterflies when they are most acting like worms! Unfortunately, we sometimes fall into the trap of expecting less of some students than others. This can happen in subtle ways, such as when teachers tell us about how a student performed last year, or we look at a student's folder of past work. I waited a few weeks to look at past test scores, preferring to learn about my students firsthand. I also chose to assume that all my students would be successful, so I refused to allow words such as "can't" to be uttered.

In *The Art and Science of Teaching*, Robert J. Marzano describes actions that are representative of lowered expectations. He compares teachers' behaviors toward high-achieving vs. low-achieving students. As he points out, teachers often exhibit different actions with students who are low-achieving. These actions include less attention; less positive interactions, such as eye contact, praise, and nonverbal cues; less wait time; fewer opportunities to answer; and less feedback and follow-up (Marzano, 2007, ASCD). In order to counter it, you can make a choice to give each student your BEST.

Give Students Your BEST
- Belief
- Encouragement
- Support
- Time

Belief

The most basic characteristic to invest in your students is a strong belief that they are important, valued, and capable. Diane Antolak, a high school principal in Fayetteville, North Carolina, explained that she personally reviews all student schedules. If she sees a student has not registered for advanced classes, and she believes the student should be in a higher level class, she changes his or her schedule, then sets up a meeting to discuss the change. As one student told me, "It makes me work harder, because I know she believes I can do the work."

If you believe in your students, you will call on each one to give them an opportunity to share a response. On p. 111, we'll discuss how you can support them to help ensure their success. You'll also stick with them when they don't know an answer. For example, if Michelle doesn't know, or stumbles with an answer, I have several possible responses. I can tell her she is wrong, call on another student to help her out, answer for her, or give up and move on to another question. However, another alternative is to use a series of questions to guide her to the correct answer. I might go to another student for help, but I continue to come back to Michelle until she demonstrates understanding. By doing so, I show her that I believe she can learn.

Encouragement

Encouragement is the wrapping paper for your present of belief. Students who do not have a lot of self-confidence need a steady stream of encouragement. Encouragement is communicated through appropriate praise and feedback, as well as nonverbal cues such as a smile. Encouragement is always a signal to the student to keep trying. It's important to encourage students regularly, especially when they are less successful. Think back to the example we just discussed. When a student is struggling to answer a question, it's important to encourage them with supportive comments while guiding them to the correct answer. Focus on their strengths to give them the confidence to continue.

Support

Providing support to accompany increased expectations is not an option. This can be as basic as guiding students through responses as in the prior example. However, it also includes ensuring that each student has access to the resources needed to accomplish more rigorous tasks. Finally, as teachers, we need to build scaffolding into projects and assignments so that students can be successful. That was the focus of chapter 5, Give Appropriate Support and Guidance.

Time

Ultimately, inspiring students through your belief, encouragement, and support requires that you make a choice to invest your time in particular students. This is evidenced in two specific ways. First, it is critical to allow appropriate wait time for every student to answer. Some students need more time to reflect before they are ready to respond. That's one of the reasons I like the strategy of Think-Pair-Share. After you ask a question, ask everyone to stop and think for approximately 45 seconds to a minute. Then, have students turn to a partner and share their responses. Finally, call on students to share their answer, or their partner's answer. Even at that point, give appropriate wait time. As a beginning teacher, if students didn't answer quickly, I was uneasy and unsure of myself. Often, I just answered for them. However, by doing that, I sent a strong message to my students that I didn't think they could answer. So my students stopped attempting to answer. Most of the time, when we think we have waited too long, we haven't.

You may also choose to pay extra attention to those students who are sometimes overlooked. In fewer than five minutes per day, you can say an extra positive comment several times during the day. Or, you can write additional feedback on a student's paper or schedule time to meet with a student during the school day to go over material he or she doesn't understand. The important part is not the amount of time you spend; it is that you commit to doing these things consistently with the students who need you.

It's Your Turn!

As you think about your students, how can you enhance what you are already doing to give each one your BEST?

Choose five of your students. List specific ways to give them your BEST.				
	Belief	*Encouragement*	*Support*	*Time*
Student:				
Student:				
Student:				
Student:				
Student:				

Expanding the Vision

It's also important to help our students expand their visions. Many of my students did not believe they could be successful. We must help them see beyond their current line of sight.

For example, you can have students tell you about their dreams for the future. You may do this through writing, or another creative outlet. Kendra Alston has her students choose or write a theme song for their lives.

Sylvia White at Reid Ross Classical School has her students create T-shirts. As a follow-up to a discussion of Martin Luther King Jr.'s life and his dream for all people, each student designs a shirt. On the front, they illustrate their dream using fabric paints, computer design graphics, or any type of embroidery. On the back, students write the steps to achieving their goal, which is based on their own research. It is an excellent way for students to learn the next steps required to achieve their goals.

In *Classroom Motivation from A to Z*, I recommend that teachers write vision letters. The task is to imagine it is the last day of school. Write a letter or e-mail to another teacher describing your year: all that your students accomplished, how they have changed, and what they learned from you. I find that writing the letter helps you define your purpose and set your priorities, which is why I had you do that as you finished chapter 1, The Case for Rigor. During my workshops, we do this activity and then discuss what that means in terms of instruction. At the end, I recommend this as also a good activity to do with students. When you ask your students to write a letter explaining why this was the best year of their lives, it helps you learn about them.

Dear Ms. Ray,

My second semester was the most successful because my mind was focused on school instead of everything else. Especially in Algebra 1 because this is a class we have to really be focused in to pass. Instead of speeding through my work like usual I took my time and reviewed my work after completing it. Even though I still had some of my mind on boys I still stayed focused on my work too.

My second semester was also successful because I let my sister help me and teach me new ways instead of arguing with her and telling her I knew what I am doing when I didn't know. I watched my cousin teach his brother different ways to do Algebra. That's why my second semester was successful.

Shakierra

Chris Webb, one of my graduate students, opened his school year with the activity.

With the letters, I wrote on the board for the kids to write why they had the most successful year in Mr. Webb's social studies class. This was the second day of school and all I had talked to them about were my rules and school rules, I had not yet done any introduction activities. I told them they only needed to write a short paragraph, not a novel, but most wrote a half-page; some wrote more. Some of the things they wrote about were not getting into any trouble, how they got into trouble and got bad grades in sixth and seventh grades and that did not happen this year, etc. It was a great activity because I got to know my students early on, and I think the kids really appreciated starting off on the right foot. I plan on keeping their letters in a file, and if students start to slip up with grades or behavior, I can pull the letter out and talk to them about it before there is a negative consequence.

Other alternatives include vision folders or vision posters. The format doesn't matter. The purpose is to give students an opportunity to express their dreams, which is the first step to expanding students' visions. You'll also want to share your own dreams as a model and to encourage them.

When possible, bring in speakers or resource materials that are linked to your students' dreams. For example, if you have a student who wants to be a painter, find a local artist to come into your classroom. If several of your students want to be pro basketball players, and you don't happen to have a pro star handy, bring in the star of the high school or college team. You'd be amazed at how much of a role model they can be for your students and how honored they are to be asked.

Finally, read stories about people and their dreams and goals for their lives. It's important to talk about men and women who achieved their dreams despite failures. By continually showing your students how other people accomplished their goals, you broaden their visions for their own lives.

Books With Stories of Successful People Who Have Overcome Failure

♦ *Great Failures of the Extremely Successful*, by Steve Young
♦ *Unstoppable*, by Cynthia Kersey
♦ *Staying With It: Role Models of Perseverance*, by Emerson Klees
♦ *The Road to Success Is Paved with Failure: How Hundreds of Famous People Triumphed Over Inauspicious Beginnings, Crushing Rejection, Humiliating Defeats and Other Speed Bumps Along Life's Highway*, by Joey Green

---

Showcasing those who have overcome obstacles is particularly important for those students who do not understand the importance of their own efforts. In *Classroom Instruction That Works* (2001), Marzano, Pickering, and Pollock make two important comments about students' views about effort.

Research-Based Generalizations About Effort

1. Not all students realize the importance of believing in effort.
2. Students can learn to change their beliefs to an emphasis on effort (Marzano et al., 2001, p. 50).

I saw this in my own classroom. Ronita, one of my students, generally struggled in class. One day, after a lot of hard work and studying, she made an A on a project. I was so proud of her, but was stunned at her response. First, she thanked me for "giving" her an A. When I told her she earned the grade, she smiled and said, "It's my lucky day." She did not realize that effort does make a difference. She thought achievement was due to an outside force, such as my help or luck. For students like Ronita, reading and learning about others whose efforts led to later success teaches them the value of their own efforts.

It's Your Turn!

First, how will you help students express their goals and dreams?

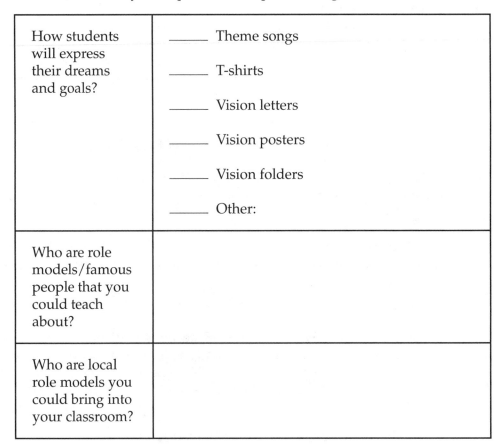

How students will express their dreams and goals?	_____ Theme songs _____ T-shirts _____ Vision letters _____ Vision posters _____ Vision folders _____ Other:
Who are role models/famous people that you could teach about?	
Who are local role models you could bring into your classroom?	

Ownership of Learning

Another way to raise expectations for students is through their ownership of learning. Student ownership is a characteristic that takes time to encourage, but you can build it by focusing on three specifics: choice, voice, and leadership.

Choice

Offering choices is one of the simplest ways to encourage student involvement in your classroom. Unfortunately, I talk to many teachers and students who don't feel as though they have any choices at all. I talked to one student who told me he felt like school was a place where "they tell you what to do all the time." Feeling a lack of choice is disheartening and frustrating for anyone. There are many opportunities for students to have choices in your classroom.

I was in an alternative school where students felt they had no choices. The English teacher was planning a unit on Shakespeare. As she and I talked, she realized that allowing her students to choose a final project would encourage stronger participation from them. However, she was uncomfortable simply letting them come up with whatever they wanted to do. She began by allowing them to explain the literary work by choosing from a list of appropriate projects, such as painting a mural, creating a music video, designing a commercial, or writing a children's book.

You could offer these options with just about any assignment you do, no matter the subject. Imagine the depth of understanding needed for a student to explain a concept in a two-minute commercial or the creativity involved in developing a blog or music video to explain content. If they are allowed to choose how they show you they understand the content, many students will invest more time and effort on the task. Project-based learning and open-ended research are both excellent options for student choice.

Voice

Student voice is actually taking the notion of choice to a higher level. With choices, you are still the primary decision maker; and you are allowing students to make some decisions, usually within some parameters. Voice is about students truly sharing in the decision-making process, and is a critical component of problem-based learning.

Adam Myers, a language arts teacher at Coulwood Middle School, used a controversial approach to spur his students to use their voices to express strong opinions. In the middle of a novel study, *Forged by Fire* by Sharon Draper (the story of a young boy's life as he attempts to protect his younger half-sister from mental, physical, and sexual abuse from their stepfather), Adam hid the books. When students asked for the books, he explained that parents were unhappy about the decision to read *Forged by Fire* and that the book was banned from the classroom because of the inappropriate subject matter in the book.

The students quickly responded: "Which parents told?" "The book isn't even that bad." "I hate this school!" "This is wrong." So he encouraged students to write letters to parents, the principal, the governor, or the president expressing how they felt about the book and what happened. All agreed that the novels belonged in their hands, no one had the right to take them away.

He then told them "I was just kidding." He explains their reaction:

I like to think of their laughter and comments about their mean teacher as relief that the books were still going to be a part of the classroom. What amazed me most . . . were the answers I received when they asked why I would do such a thing. It was in this conversation with my students that I saw that I had truly used literature and writing to help my students both academically and developmentally. They were attached to the characters and felt cheated that they wouldn't know the end of the plot. They took ownership of their writing as they justified that although the novel was controversial, it allowed them to explore a realistic situation that unfortunately was too close to some of their friends, classmates, or family members. My students have not forgiven me, and that is o.k. because I'm sure they will never forget me.

What a powerful lesson. He tapped into students' strong feelings of justice and choice with a real-life example of censorship to spark ownership of an issue. Although a controversial activity, it clearly had a lasting impact on his students.

Leadership

A final way to build ownership is to provide opportunities for each student to be a leader in your room. I think the best, most consistent examples of this happen in early childhood classrooms. There is a leader for the day listed on the board. Or there is a chart on the board and it lists the leaders for the day: the lunch line leader, the calendar leader, the recess leader, and so on. Every child has a specific role, and the teacher rotates those regularly. In that particular classroom, everyone is a leader at least once a week.

Allowing students the chance to be in charge is an important part of education. And for some of your students, your classroom is the only place they are given that opportunity. Gin Sorrow shared: "I had some very social and unmotivated girls that were negative leaders in a class. I challenged them to teach the next section. They would come early in the mornings and work with me during planning times to prepare the lessons. It was a wonderful experience. I was able to see some of their methods for connecting with their peers that I could incorporate in to my teaching the rest of the year. The girls grew into more positive leaders and challenged the other students to improve. It is definitely a strategy I would use again."

Many teachers use more formal structures, such as electing class officers. There was a story in our local paper about a fifth grader who was constantly in and out of trouble. After three suspensions, his teacher decided to take a different approach. She held an election, he was voted class president, and his whole attitude changed.

Tamara Willis, seventh-grade social studies teacher at Sullivan Middle School chose a similar approach after her students complained, "School is like a job and... we should get paid for attending." They voted to create a business, which was named Sullivan University. Students prepared resumes and applied for positions (Dean, Professor, and Intern) and interviewed one another for the jobs. Those students who were hired to be deans held an executive board meeting with Ms. Willis to form teams and design new classroom rules to address issues related to poor behavior and absenteeism.

As the experiment continued, students began to demonstrate leadership by quieting their peers when they were disruptive. The result? Attendance increased, students were more engaged in instruction, and discipline referrals decreased. All these examples have one thing in common: The teachers chose to channel students' negative behaviors into positive action.

Ultimately, you have the final say in your classroom. After all, you are the teacher. But if you are willing to share that ownership with your students to create a true community of learners, you will also reap the benefits. Not only will your students want to come to class, so will you.

Try It Out!

	I'd like to try . . .
Choice	
Voice	
Leadership	

Tracking Progress

As you increase expectations, it's important to help students see that they are making progress. Remember, one of the two cornerstones of motivation is how a person feels about success. As we discussed in chapter 2, Digging Into Rigor, seeing progress toward a larger goal helps us build a sense of competence and achievement, which leads to increased self-confidence, which then gives us courage to keep going. Although we are talking about students tracking their own progress here through evaluation and self-reflection, it is also important to remember that as teachers, we use what we learn about our students to adjust our future instruction. That's the formative part of an overall assessment plan, which differs from the use of grades for evaluation.

We're going to specifically talk about tracking progress in learning, but the same principles apply to tracking other types of progress, such as behavior. You can do this formally or informally. I visited Reid Ross Classical School in Fayetteville, North Carolina, and was impressed at the depth of commitment the teachers and students show toward tracking growth. Through weekly growth tests, teachers continually assess their students' content knowledge. More importantly, the students track their own growth weekly in a journal. Diane Antolak, principal at Reid Ross, notes that her experience as a marathon runner led to her idea for the growth tests. ". . . if we track our progress physically and that helps us train better and more efficiently, why wouldn't we do that in learning also?"

Kendra Alston chooses to use writing to help her students track progress. She asks students to continually reflect on their learning in notebooks. Then, she asks them to write a reflection on their learning at the end of the nine weeks. Through the process, students began to understand how they can be successful, which provides a base for additional growth. Reflective writing, by the way, is one of the routine writing tasks specified by the CCSS.

Sample Reflections

"Over this quarter, I've learned many things. One thing I've learned is teachers mean business and don't take kindly to slacking. I found that out the hard way. Another thing is that if you take the time to listen, teachers have a lot of helpful tips for passing the school year."

—*Justin, end of first 9 weeks*

"Something else that I learn (sic) would be about text organizers such as title, headings, caption/photograph, sidebars, and tags. Text organizers were not that confusing. At first I was getting tags and headings mixed up, but shortly I begin to understand them by the hands-on labs . . . I found that I understand the lessons better when we are able to do hands-on and get to experience and find what it is about ourselves."

—*Malissa, end of first 9 weeks*

"This school year has been unexplainable. I have improved so much over this past year I don't know where to begin . . . For once I actually worked hard on my work. Instead of waiting till the last minute to do work I had to start right when it was given. I learned that the harder you work on an assignment, the more likely you will get a good grade."

—*Karina, end of year*

I encourage students to keep a "Victory List" in their agendas or notebooks. A Victory List is simply a personal list of successes that can help us remember what we have accomplished, particularly when things aren't going so well. I do this with my graduate students all the time. They will come in to see me, worried about an assignment, particularly if there's a lot going on in their schools and they are feeling pressed for time. After they finish talking, I remind them of all the other assignments they successfully completed; then I say, "I know you can do this one too. After all, you did well on all the others, and they were also difficult. If you could do them, you can do this one too." Sometimes when we're struggling, we forget all that we've accomplished.

Periodically, I use a Stop and Go approach to reflecting on progress. First, I ask students to STOP.

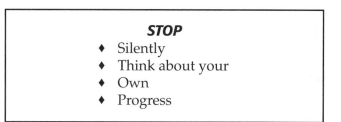

Then, I ask them to GO, by charting areas where they still need to grow (things they don't understand or need to learn more about) and areas where they are "on top of it."

Growth opportunities	On top of it

A final way to involve students in tracking their own progress is through student-led conferences. Instead of the typical parent-teacher conference, where the teacher tells the parents how their son or daughter is doing in class, the student is an active participant-leader. Prior to the conference, the student meets with the teacher to determine particular items to show during the conference. Then, during the conference, the student explains what he or she has learned, using the work samples as evidence. Parents are encouraged to listen and ask questions of their son or daughter, and the teacher serves as a facilitator of the conversation. Student-led conferences develop a sense of ownership in students and parents, since they are personally involved in the process, as opposed to simply being told what is happening.

It's Your Turn!

Identify several students who have probably never experienced the Success Cycle. How will you help them track their progress?

Ideas for Helping Students Track Progress	
Tracking Growth in Scores	
Victory List	
Stop and Go Reflection	
Student-Led Conferences	

Creating a Culture

As we discussed in chapter 1, rigor is creating an environment in which each student is expected to learn at high levels, each student is supported so he or she can learn at high levels, and each student demonstrates learning at high levels. To do that, you must create a culture of high expectations. Changing a culture doesn't happen overnight; but if you are consistent, you will see a difference. Much of what we've already discussed helps you build the culture you want, but let's look at one or two other possibilities.

One of the basic ways to encourage high expectations is to refuse to allow any statement that reflects lowered beliefs. I never allowed students to use the phrase "I can't" in my classroom. You may choose not to try or you may not want to or you may not be there yet, but saying you can't simply isn't an option. It took several weeks, but then the students really bought into it. Again, I am unable to "make" you believe in yourself, but I absolutely refuse to reinforce your lack of belief.

Belief-building is critical. I have a strong belief that I can tackle any challenge. A friend asked me how I became so confident—where or when did I get my belief that I could achieve my dreams? My belief in myself is built on a strong base of memories. First, I have countless memories of people who believed in me and shared that belief with me. My parents, my grandparents, former teachers, friends; the list is long. Their encouragement helped me learn to believe in myself, even when I wasn't successful with a project. Second, based on their support, many times I persisted through failure until I succeeded. Then, the memories of my successes give me the strength to attempt the next challenge.

Your students need the same memories. They will remember the times you show them you believe in them. But they sometimes forget the successes they achieve. That's why it's important to track progress, which allows them to build their own memory base. And, as your students continue to achieve success, they will begin to encourage each other, rather than looking only to you.

Finally, use your environment to reinforce your culture. Post motivating quotes. As we discussed on page 115, read and write about people who have overcome adversity. Bring in role models. Talk about your dreams, your successes, and your mistakes. Show your students they can be more than they are. Over time, they will believe you!

It's Your Turn!

How do you want to change the culture in your room? What do you want out of your class (words such as *can't*)? What do you want in your class (quotes, etc.)?

Words I Want to Exclude from My Classroom	Things I Want to Include in My Classroom

Conclusion

Raised expectations are the heart of a rigorous classroom. It begins and ends with you. What are the expectations you have for yourself and your students? How do you share those and help your students expand their beliefs about themselves? By setting the standard that all students can and will learn and helping them see their progress, your students will grow to new heights of learning. And then, you will have created a new culture!

Final Insights

- The most important idea I read was . . .

- One way I plan to apply this information in my classroom is . . .

- I wonder . . .

8

Assessment and Grading

In the preceding chapters, we have discussed a wide range of strategies you can incorporate into your lessons to increase rigor. Many of those learning activities result in a product that can be used to assess learning. Now, we'll shift our attention to the critical aspects of evaluation and assessment. I've found that nothing derails attempts at rigor as quickly as problems with grading. Yet, before we talk about grades, we should discuss the aspect of assessment that can have a greater impact on student learning, formative assessment.

Assessment That Impacts Learning

Formative assessment is one of the hottest buzzwords in education today. A google search nets over a quarter of a million hits! I strongly believe that if we are going to truly support our students to higher levels, we must continually assess their learning and use that information to plan our future instruction. In 1998, Black and Wiliam provided a clear rationale that using formative assessment effectively raises standards. In 2004, they and other researchers provided a fuller explanation of formative assessment in *Working Inside the Black Box: Assessment for Learning in the Classroom.*

Assessment for learning is any assessment for which the first priority in its design and practice is to serve the purpose of promoting pupils' learning. It thus differs from assessment designed primarily to serve the purposes of accountability or of ranking or of certifying competence. An assessment activity can help learning if it provides information to be used as feedback, by teachers, and by their pupils, in assessing themselves and each other, to modify the teaching and learning activities in which they are engaged. (Black et al., 2004)

What does that mean to you as you consider your current assessments, whether they are tests, projects, homework, or a mix of items? Let's back up for a minute. Many assessments used in classrooms are summative. In other words, they are used to evaluate a student. We will discuss that more in terms of grading later in this chapter. However, formative assessments are used to help a student and teacher adjust to improve learning. Amy Benjamin (2008) provides a helpful comparison.

Formative and Summative Assessments Compared

Formative Assessment	Summative Assessment
Student is aware of the questions throughout the assessment process	Questions on a test are surprises to the student
Timing is flexible	Student must perform within time limits
Teacher's feedback is commentary and/or letter or number grade	Teacher's feedback is a letter or number grade
Evaluation is used to guide future learning	Evaluation is used to rank and sort students
Considers the student's zone of proximal development	Does not consider the student as an individual learner
Test or task may be flexible	Test or task is not flexible
Student is involved in self-assessment	Assessment by teacher or outside agency only
Sets reachable targets for future learning	No direct follow-up; when it's over, it's over.
Results are not used as a report card grade	Results figure in to the report card grade

If you teach in a school where grades are the only purpose of assessment, this concept may be new to you. W. James Popham (2008) in *Transformative Assessment*, describes four levels of implementation. As with anything new, don't try to jump in on the deep end.

Popham's Levels	
Level One	Calls for teachers to use formative assessment to collect evidence by which they can adjust their current and future instructional activities.
Level Two	Deals with students' use of formative assessment evidence to adjust their own learning tactics.
Level Three	Represents a complete change in the culture of a classroom, shifting the overriding role of classroom assessment from the means to compare students with one another for grade assignments to the means to generate evidence from which teachers and students can, if warranted, adjust what they're doing.
Level Four	Consists of a schoolwide adoption of one or more levels of formative assessment, chiefly through the use of professional development and teacher learning communities.

Source: Popham (2008, p. ix).

Using Formative Assessment to Fuel Your Instruction

As I have done throughout this book, we will place our emphasis on what you can do in your classroom. In *Literacy from A to Z* (2008), I describe formative assessment as a three-step process: look at your students to learn about them, watch their progress, and help them grow.

> ### Three-Step Process of Formative Assessment
> ♦ Look at your students to learn about them.
> ♦ Watch their progress.
> ♦ Help them grow.

There are many ways you can gather data and use it to design instruction. We will not take the time to fully investigate formative assessment; that would take an entire book. For our purposes, simply recognize that the instructional strategies described throughout this book are excellent ways to determine if your students are learning. For example, in chapter 4, Increase Complexity, we discussed ways to assess background knowledge. That is one way to *look at your students to learn about them.*

Next, you should *watch their progress.* In chapter 7, Raise Expectations, we discussed ways your students can track their own progress. Now, let me give you two quick ways to informally assess your students' progress in any area. When I was teaching, I collected my data in a simple chart and coded the boxes with either a check plus (total mastery), check (mastery, but review is needed), check minus (partial understanding), or minus (minimal or no understanding). That allowed me to scan to see individual students' needs, but also to see students who needed to be grouped together for additional instruction.

Student	*Skill/Objective*	*Skill/Objective*	*Skill/Objective*
Chad	✓	✓+	✓+
Katrina	—	✓	✓
José	—	✓	✓

Kendra Alston used a similar checklist format, but she color-coded her observations of students: Green (Go Ahead), Yellow (Slow Down and Review), Red (Stop for Much More Work).

Again, the format can be anything that helps you understand where your students are performing. Notice I said "that helps you understand. . . ." Too often, we have information, but don't use it to plan instruction. For example, if you use the graphic organizer for teaching vocabulary in chapter 4, Increase Complexity, and find that your students struggle with examples and nonexamples, formative assessment demands that you plan instruction to address that need. Data is just a set of numbers or comments unless you use it to make a difference in learning. And that is the critical difference with formative assessment. Its main purpose is to *help your students GROW.*

> **Help Students GROW**
>
> G—Gauge where your students are.
> R—Recognize their strengths and weaknesses.
> O—One step at a time, provide instruction to help them grow.
> W—Watch them rise to higher levels.

It's Your Turn!

How do you currently assess students? How do you use that information to plan or adjust your instruction? What is one way you can use formative assessment in your classroom?

_____

_____

_____

_____

_____

Grading Practices

Formative assessment is a critical part of our instruction. But there is also the evaluative portion, the assigning of grades as a designator of success in learning. I've found that grading is one of the most controversial aspects of teaching, and it can be an immediate roadblock to increasing rigor. As one teacher recently said to me, "The only thing my students and their parents care about is an A. They don't want rigor if it means lower grades." And with the Common Core's emphasis on text complexity across the curriculum, concerns about how to grade in this challenging environment are valid.

In *Developing Grading and Reporting Systems for Student Learning* (2001), Thomas R. Guskey and Jane M. Bailey describe six major purposes of grading and reporting:

1. Communicate achievement status;
2. Provide information students can use for self-evaluation;
3. Select, identify, or group students;
4. Provide incentives for students to learn;
5. Evaluate effectiveness of instructional programs; and
6. Provide evidence of students' lack of effort or responsibility. (p. 51)

Each of these purposes is acceptable, but often we don't think about why we use grades. We simply assume that grades exist for a reason, and we may not challenge something that is accepted as the norm.

It's Your Turn!
What is your major purpose for grading?

_____

_____

_____

_____

_____

Perspectives on Grading

Grading is another topic that deserves more attention than we can address here. There are many valuable resources available, and I've listed several in the recommended resource section at the end of the book. For now, we are taking a beginning look at the issues surrounding grading, to prompt your thinking toward possible changes in your own practice. In *How to Grade for Learning* (2002), Ken O'Conner provides seven perspectives that add depth to our consideration of grading.

O'Conner's Seven Perspectives on Grading	
Perspective One	Grading is not essential for learning.
Perspective Two	Grading is complicated.
Perspective Three	Grading is subjective and emotional.
Perspective Four	Grading is inescapable.
Perspective Five	Grading has a limited research base.
Perspective Six	Grading has no single best practice.

(continued)

Perspective Seven	Grading that is faulty damages students and teachers.

When I started teaching elementary and junior high school, evaluating students was a struggle. I was never sure if I was doing it correctly, or if there was one correct way to evaluate and grade. Advice from colleagues was pretty simple: be able to back up anything you put down as a grade, and save everything. I kept a file of student folders, which included every paper or test that was graded. I mainly used them if a parent or a student questioned a grade. As I look back on that experience, I see how focused I was on the wrong thing, particularly since those files were a treasure chest of information with far more potent uses.

During that period, I looked on grading as having to prove that my opinion (the grade) was correct. I felt as though I was on the defensive, and, as a result, grading was my least favorite task. I wish I had read these principles then, because they would have helped me understand how to use grades more effectively.

However, a different set of circumstances helped me. After I started teaching remedial students, grades mattered differently to my students. In fact, they didn't matter much at all, so I shifted my attention. I thought about why I graded something, how I graded it, and lastly, how I could explain it to my students and parents in a way that would help them see why learning was important. As a result, my evaluation of students and the grading process became more authentic and valuable to me and my students.

Grading Without Guilt

Out of my experiences, I've come to realize that, although there is no perfect way to grade, there are steps we can take to minimize the negative aspects of grading.

> ### *Minimizing Negative Aspects of Grading*
> - Recognize the value of grading to students, parents, and others.
> - Shift the emphasis to learning.
> - Provide clear guidelines.
> - Require quality work.
> - Communicate clearly.
> - Be patient.

Recognize Value

First, recognize why grades are valued. Some students want good grades because they are looking for outside affirmation that they are worthy. Others need a high grade point average for college admission and/or scholarships. Still others enjoy the competition of comparing themselves to others. Understanding why a student or parent is concerned about grading will help you communicate more effectively. As I've said before, value is one of the two driving forces of motivation. That applies to grades also.

It's Your Turn!

For each group listed, what is the value of grades?

Value for Students	
Value for Parents	
Value for Teachers	
Other Value?	

Shift the Emphasis

Next, shift the emphasis to learning as opposed to grades. This takes time, and I'm not sure you can ever get students or parents to completely ignore grades, but you can de-emphasize them. Think of it like a seesaw with learning on one end and grades on the other. At a minimum, you want it to be balanced evenly. Ideally, you can tilt it a little toward learning. If you think back to the discussion on formative assessment, learning was the priority. So, the more you use formative assessment, the more you tilt toward the learning end of the seesaw.

One of the quickest and most effective methods I've used for minimizing a focus on grades is to have a large number of grades. That may seem counterintuitive, but when students receive a final grade based on one or two big items, such as tests or projects, it heightens anxiety. When a student has a larger number and wide variety of opportunities to demonstrate understanding, one bad grade does not matter as much. It's a choice of making every grade high-stakes versus giving students multiple opportunities to be successful.

Provide Clear Guidelines

I also provided students with clear guidelines and a detailed rubric for all projects and key assignments. It is not fair to students to ask them to guess about our expectations for quality. A particular issue for many students is that they don't know what "good" looks like. We ask students to complete an assignment, and then we are frustrated when the quality of work does not match our expectations as teachers. This leads us to question whether or not the student cares about doing the work ("He or she just isn't motivated") or to wonder if the student tried at all ("If he or she tried, they would have done better"). But, for many of our most frustrated, and frustrating students, they simply don't know what to do, or how to do it, or they think what they are doing it right!

As Bob Heath, principal of Sullivan Middle School points out,

It's important to set up what a good grade is. How does a student know what an A is? A student should be able to write a paper and say, "Can I myself look at it and see if I wrote an A paper?" Setting up clear assessments well in advance is part of raising the bar. Sometimes we artificially raise the bar by just making it harder and not providing kids advanced, clear guidelines as to what it takes to achieve. Grades go down, but that isn't real rigor.

You might want to refer back to chapter 5, Give Appropriate Support and Guidance. That's where we talked about providing clear guidelines for students and helping them understand our expectations. For any major assignment that is graded, I suggest you use a clear, detailed rubric that includes a description of your expectations.

Sample Expectation Categories for Rubrics

- ♦ Components to be included.
- ♦ Quality of content.
- ♦ Organization of material.
- ♦ Presentation of material.
- ♦ Grammar, conventions, and readability of material.

Learning Is Not Optional

I regularly hear from teachers who tell me they have high standards, explaining that any student who doesn't turn in homework or a project receives a zero. Although that policy may send a strong message about meeting deadlines, I believe that allowing students to take a zero reflects lower expectations. It permits a student to get by without actually doing the work and says to the student, "You don't have to learn this. It's okay to take a zero and get off the hook for learning."

If something is important enough for you to assign it, then it should be important enough for a student to complete it. Let me clarify a key point. This is not just about the student's responsibility. You play a major role in his or her success. First, it means we design assignments that are valuable, not just busy work. In addition to helping students understand the value of the work, we hold them responsible for completion.

When I was teaching, that meant that students who did not complete homework stayed with me during lunch and completed it while eating. You don't have to give up your lunch time, but requiring students to complete something means you also provide a structure and support to ensure they finish. I was recently in a high school where the teachers posted office hours for students to receive extra help. That's a great idea, but the students who need the most help usually don't voluntarily seek it. Another school in the same district offered specified times for help, but it was required for any student who failed a test. The teachers sent a clear message that learning was not a choice.

I took several teachers and the principal from a local school to visit a high-poverty school in a neighboring state. The school had a strong reputation for closing achievement gaps, despite the challenging student population. Bob Heath, the principal of our local middle school, described his experience.

> The option to not do work was not there at Reid Ross. If as adults, we accept that students cannot do work, we are not doing the kids any service at all. This comes out in several ways, starting with our vocabulary. If we say "students just won't do the work," we are part of the problem. We have to get those words out of our vocabulary. They won't do because we don't make them do.

When you require students to finish an assignment at an acceptable level, you communicate that you believe they can complete the work. Increased expectations lead to increased rigor. Bob agrees, continuing,

The problem is that we take a one-dimensional approach to a three-dimensional problem. For example, we tell teachers we want increased rigor. But we also tell teachers you can't give students a zero if they didn't do it, you can only give them a 60. Teachers say "Where's the authenticity of that?" That is the one-dimensional view, saying "I can't give them what they earn, which is nothing." My response as a principal is that we forget to take the next step—if you don't give them a zero, what do you do? True rigor is providing another opportunity or additional information to help the student learn and do what they didn't do. We need to build that into the process. If we raise the bar to have rigor then we need to provide something for the kids that aren't quite ready. Some need extra help, some aren't motivated, and we need to deal with those issues. The main grading issue of rigor is that if we raise the bar, we automatically begin to leave some kids behind unless we provide some stopgaps.

Wow! That's a challenge. Many of my graduate students teach in school systems that do not allow zeroes. I agree with the purpose of that policy. Too often, students receive zeroes early in the year and they fall so far behind, they can never catch up. And again, it allows students to choose to fail, which goes against everything I believe. But I cannot support simply writing down a score of 60 when a student has not completed any work. In Bob's school, over time, they have made progress toward a solution.

What we have discovered here is that just teaching more isn't what raises the bar. It's making kids do the work that they are hesitating or refusing to do. We created more time in our daily schedule for students to get face-to-face with teachers to complete that work. If they don't turn something in, they meet with that teacher to do the assignment. They are not going to get away with just not doing it. We have to break the cycle of passive resistance a lot of kids have toward doing work. It's developed over years but we have to say "No." We are going to make you do the work. We will not just give you a 60. We will make you do the work to earn the authentic grade.

Bob's suggestions are excellent, but they are working in part because it is a schoolwide expectation. The use of a "Not Yet" or "Incomplete" policy for projects and assignments shifts the emphasis to learning and allows students to revise and resubmit work until it is at an acceptable level. Requiring quality work, work that meets the teachers expectations, lets students know that the priority is learning, not simple completion of an assignment.

Recently, I had the opportunity to speak with Toni Eubank of the Southern Regional Education Board (SREB). As part of their comprehensive school reform model, SREB has long been a proponent of holding students to high expectations for completed work. She describes the model as Instant Credit Recovery (or Instant Content Recovery for middle school students).

This grading intervention practice requires that teachers rethink credit recovery completely. If it is okay for students to retake courses to meet standards, why is it not okay to retake tests that do not meet standards, revise essays, redo classwork and homework that do not meet standards? Why do we let students "off the hook" for learning and for completing work that meets the standards during our classes, and then spend thousands and thousands of dollars requiring them to retake entire courses they have failed, many simply because they did not do homework? Instead of sitting in classes throughout the semester or year putting forth little to no effort, doing little work, failing tests or turning in garbage instead of high-quality work, students must now be required to work as they go. This method truly reflects job-embedded skills and habits and better prepares students for college and careers. Instead of retaking courses and earning credit (often for seat time only) in our current credit recovery programs, students must now work while they go—sort of a "pay as you go" method. (Eubank, 2011, p. 1)

Eight Key Elements of the Instant Credit Recovery Model (Eubank, 2011)
1. Teachers no longer assign grades below a C.
2. Eliminate the use of zeros.
3. Late work is late, but it must be completed if teachers are to correctly determine if students know, understand, and are able to do whatever the verb within the standard calls for.
4. Students must be given extra help opportunities (required) to learn the information, skill, or concept to complete assignments.
5. Students must retake tests that they fail and redo all assignments they earn less than a C grade on.
6. Consequences change for students not having work ready to turn in on time.
7. Grading systems change from zeros or failing grades to "I's" or some other form of non-grade.
8. A few students will still fail no matter what. The goal is to get MORE students to complete MORE assignments and assessments to the proficient level of the standard.

In my university classroom, I used a grading policy with a three-part scale: A, B, and Not Yet. If my graduate students were unable to complete a project at an acceptable level (B or above), then they received a Not Yet and revise their work. Originally, my students thought that meant I was easier on grading. The first night, I usually heard someone say, "Wow, this means the worst I can do is a B. That is great." For those students whose work was not at an acceptable level, I required them to meet with me and come up with a plan for revising the work. Then I set a deadline for the revision. It's at that point that my students realized the policy wasn't easy—it was more challenging.

Since they are all teachers, it's usually one of those moments they learned more than content; they learned a process to use in their own classrooms. By the end of the semester, they had an entirely different attitude about learning and grading. As one of my students told me, "I didn't really like your Not Yet policy, but then I realized you were teaching us to focus on learning, not on a grade. I'm going to try to do the same thing with my students." When you require students to finish an assignment at an acceptable level, you show them you believe they can successfully complete the work.

Robin Madden, a teacher in Rock Hill, South Carolina, shares a pilot grading policy developed by teachers at Saluda Trail Middle School and South Pointe High School. It focuses on allowing students to revise summative and formative assignments for reassessment.

Sample Reassessment Policy

- ◆ Students are provided at least one re-assessment opportunity per major task/assessment.
- ◆ When reassessment is offered, all students may be reassessed, regardless of the grade on the original task/assessment. In other words, all students may retake summative or formative assessments, as long as they relearn the material first.
- ◆ Students who cheat are also allowed to retake, but they're docked 20 percent and a written administrative referral.
- ◆ The reassessment grade should replace the original grade if it is higher than the original grade. Students are assigned the higher of the two grades.

Another alternative is to provide a structured opportunity to improve learning. Abbigail Armstrong, a former middle school teacher, now teaches undergraduate students at a local university. As she graded a set of tests, answers to one particular question jumped out at her. The students had made significant mistakes, and clearly did not understand the content. She realized that she had not covered the material as well as she thought. Rather than simply failing everyone in the class, she looked for an alternative to ensure understanding. As a part of their mid-term exam, she required her students to complete a question in a take-home testing format. Using any course materials, they had to revisit the prior test question and correct or clarify any incorrect or incomplete information. They also identified new information they believed they should have included in their original essays.

There was a key benefit of this process: her students viewed the tests differently. As one stated, "You didn't just give me a grade; if you had, I would just know that my answer is incorrect but I wouldn't do anything about it." Another pointed out, "We had to look up the incorrect information ourselves, so we will remember." Her students took ownership of their learning. And, rather than simply restating the question on the second test, she reframed it in a way that encouraged depth of understanding.

I would like to give you one more alternative to requiring quality work, one that is a bit simpler. Lindsay Grant and Christy Matkovich incorporate opportunities in their math class for students to demonstrate they truly understand the content. Students are given the opportunity to rework any problems that were incorrect on a test (see p. 139).

However, as the graphic organizer shows, students are also asked to think about their learning by explaining why they missed the original question, and why they know they have the correct answer now. As Lindsay explains, the process "makes them think about what they've done and what they did differently or what they are supposed to do." Partial credit is added to the student's score. You might argue that they are rewarding effort, and that is true to a degree. In any type of Not Yet policy, even this example, the student who is willing to redo the assignment or missed questions has a potential reward. However, they still must rework the problem correctly to gain points. Effort is important, but quality of work is graded.

Understanding Math Better

Name _____   Date _____

Math Test _____   Teacher _____

Question:

My Original Answer:

My New Solution (you must show your work including all steps):

The Correct Answer:

Why I Missed the Question on the Original Test (circle one):

   I didn't understand the question.

   I thought I had it right.

   I skipped a step.

   I studied this but I forgot.

   I had no clue about this.

   I ran out of time or guessed.

   I made a careless mistake.

Why I Know I Have the Right Answer Now:

Try It Out!

Think about the options for grading. Which appeal to you?

	How I already do this	*What I'd like to try*
Instant Credit Recovery		
Not Yet Grading		
Reassessment/ Retaking of Tests		

Communicate Clearly

In addition, provide clear communication about your grades. I believe it is critical to have a clear explanation for your philosophy and/or policy about grading. If homework "counts," students and parents need to know that. Ms. Keith does not grade homework, but if a student neglects to turn it in she takes points off the final grade. She believes that students need to do homework for the sake of learning, and then their grades on tests will be higher because of the homework. That is fine, but she never told her students. When Jorge made a C, despite test grades that averaged to a B, his parents called to question the overall grade. They finally understood, but commented to the principal, "It would have been okay if we had just known." The last thing you want to hear from a student or a parent is, "If

I had just known. . . ." One of the school districts I work with requires all teachers to provide a written grading policy. They don't dictate the terms of the policy; they believe teachers should have that choice. However, all teachers must have a written explanation of what and how they grade, and provide reminders to students of the policies.

Sample Grading Policy Components

- Description of Types of Assessments (tests, projects, homework, etc.)
- Description of Weight of Assessments (percentage of grade, etc.)
- Overall Expectations for Completion (e.g., Not Yet policy for projects)
- Procedures for Makeup Work (when student is absent)
- Opportunities for Extra Help (regularly scheduled days and times)

Be Patient

Finally, be patient. Although I struggle less with grades now than I did as a first year teacher, I can't tell you that grading is easy. Graduate students are entirely different creatures when it comes to grades. Every semester, I have at least one discussion with a student who is upset over his or her grade, typically because he or she made a B instead of an A! If I had my choice, I'd love to teach in a situation with no grades. However, for most of us, grading is a reality we must live with. Remember, the "Not Yet" policy also applies to you! If your initial attempt with grading or rigor doesn't go as smoothly as you would like, take time to reflect and readjust rather than giving up.

Notice I am not giving you a lockstep method for grading. Although grading is a public decision, since the results are always shared with at least one other person, I believe decisions about grading are intensely personal, a reflection of who you are and what you believe about learning. I won't give you a formula that tells you exactly what to use each time you need to evaluate your students. However, the principles we've discussed can help you plan.

Principles for Evaluation and Grading

- Use a variety of assessments.
- Make sure the type of assessment matches your purpose.
- Clearly explain what you are evaluating and the purpose of the evaluation.
- Create and provide explicit guidelines for grading.
- Build in opportunities for students to succeed.

It's Your Turn!

Think about your current grading policies and procedures. Are there changes you can make to shift the focus more toward learning and less toward the grade itself?

Idea	*How I Can Make This Work In My Classroom*
Develop a written explanation of grading policy for parents and students.	
Increase number of assessments for grading.	
Increase variety of assessments.	
Provide rubrics or other explanations of grades for key assignments.	
Incorporate a Not Yet policy for major projects.	
Another idea I have:	

Conclusion

Assessment and grading are critical cornerstones in a rigorous classroom. Often, we find that grading consumes our attention, yet formative assessment has more potential for impacting our students' learning. As you increase rigor in your expectations for learning, be sure to align your evaluation and assessments in a similar manner.

Final Insights

♦ The most important idea I read was . . .

♦ One way I plan to apply this information in my classroom is . . .

♦ I wonder . . .

9

Collaboration and Professional Learning Communities

An important part of raising the level of rigor in your classroom and school is collaborating with other teachers. There are various options and purposes for working together.

Professional Learning Communities

Many teachers are members of professional learning communities. The term has become so commonplace that it can mean any type of collaboration.

The original meaning of a professional community of learners reflected the commitment of teachers and leaders who continuously seek to grow professionally and act upon their new learning.

There are three defining characteristics of PLCs. First, professional learning communities are focused on student learning. As Dufour (2006) promotes, the goal is to improve student learning by improving what you do in the classroom.

Next, there is a culture of collaboration among the participants. You've probably worked in or seen a team of teachers who were assigned to a task, each performed their part of the tasked, and then they walked away. That's not a true PLC. In a PLC, teachers collaborate to move beyond tasks and learn together.

Options for Professional Learning Communities

Interdisciplinary Teams	Subject Area Teams
Grade Level Teams	Special Topic Teams
Vertical Teams	

Finally, professional learning communities focus on results, no matter what it takes. Although there may be a discussion of challenges, they are not used as excuses.

Successful professional learning communities provide time for you and other teachers to talk about curriculum and instruction, examine data about student learning, and plan for instructional improvements. For instance, in light of the Common Core guidelines for emphasizing the reading of informational texts across the subject areas, PLCs offer an opportunity to collaborate with teachers in multiple disciplines to identify and even share the teaching of appropriate texts.

It's Your Turn!

Self-Assess Your Willingness to Participate in a PLC

Willingness to Participate in a PLC	Yes/No (Why or Why Not)
I want to use my knowledge and skills to help other teachers.	
I want other teachers to share their knowledge and skills to help me improve my teaching.	
I am willing to participate in and promote open, honest communication.	
I will participate in a collaboration that is focused on improving student learning, building shared knowledge about best practice, and making a difference in terms of results, no matter what.	
I will honor my commitments to members of my PLC.	

(continued)

I want to analyze student work at a higher level, set goals based on that data, and implement effective teaching practices to meet those goals.	
I am willing to try and adapt new instructional practices, even if they are not successful the first time.	
I will help establish team goals, norms, and protocols to ensure collaborative work, and participate in adjustments needed to ensure this focus.	

Activities for Professional Learning Communities

Although there are many ways for PLCs to work together, we are going to take a look at five of the most common.

> ### Five Activities for Professional Learning Communities
> 1. Book Studies
> 2. Developing Consistent Expectations
> 3. Learning Walks
> 4. Lesson Studies
> 5. Looking at Student Work

Book Studies

One way to engage with other teachers to learn about a topic is to participate in a book study. Book studies allow everyone to read the same book, discuss the content, and evaluate its impact of instruction. Throughout the process, teachers can implement some of the recommendations in the book, and talk about the classroom results.

There are several strategies you can use to help your book study be more effective. First, the group should agree on standard norms of participation, such as meeting times, expectations for reading and implementation, and what will happen after the book is read.

Next, choose a facilitator whose role is to facilitate the group meeting. Third, choose a book with a clear objective that matches the PLC's goals based on an analysis of data. For example, if your student data shows a need for emphasizing writing across the curriculum, then find a book on the same topic.

Finally, remember that conversation is a critical aspect of the book study. Each member of the group should have an opportunity to share insights, ask questions about the material, and learn from others. Before you start a study, it is important to talk about how the material will be applied in each teacher's classroom and how to overcome any potential obstacles to effective communication.

Try It Out!

What areas would you like to focus on for classroom improvement? What books might help you with this?

_____

_____

_____

Developing Consistent Expectations

Another excellent activity for professional learning communities is to develop consistent expectations. For example, many teachers work together to develop common expectations for grading. As we discussed in chapter 8, Assessment and Grading, it is helpful to have a clear grading policy to provide information to students and parents.

Even though an individual teacher can (and should) develop a policy, developing consistency across teachers can help you more effectively deal with the challenges related to grading and rigor.

Learning Walks

Learning walks provide a "snapshot" of what is happening in classrooms. They are not used for evaluative purposes or for individual feedback; rather, their purpose is to help teachers learn about overall instruction.

Additionally, the goal is to identify areas of instructional strengths, as well as possible challenges.

Keep in mind that, since you are dropping in and out of classrooms, you are looking for overall patterns within a grade level, subject area, or school. You may also want to begin with looking for positive examples, in order to build trust.

A school in Chicago organized "I Spy" days. Teachers dropped in on classrooms for 5-10 minutes in order to identify positive examples of instruction. Teachers came back together after school with their "detective notebooks" to share what they had seen. It was an invigorating experience for teachers, who said this was the first time they had a chance to look at other classrooms. As one teacher explained, "I don't get time to visit other teachers' classes. I learned so much, and I have two new ideas I want to implement tomorrow."

Lesson Studies

Lesson studies emphasize working in small groups to plan, teach, observe, and critique a lesson. It's an excellent reflection of the principles of professional learning communities, as the goal is to systematically examine your teaching in order to become more effective.

In a lesson study, teachers work together to develop a detailed plan for a lesson. One member of the group teaches the lesson to his or her students, while other members of the group observe. Next, the group discusses their observations about the lesson and student learning.

Teachers revise the lesson based on their observations, then a second group member teaches the lesson, with other members once again observing. Then, the group meets to discuss the revised lesson. Finally, teachers talk about what the study lesson taught them and how they can apply the learning in their own classroom.

Looking at Student Work

A final way to improve classroom instruction is to look at authentic student work. When you examine and evaluate student work, you can clarify your own standards for work, strengthen common expectations for students, or align curriculum across classrooms.

It's important that the discussion is focused on results, not on personalities. At the beginning of the process, agree on a process for the discussion. One of my favorite websites, www.lasw.org, provides a variety and tools for looking at student work.

The "Tuning Protocol" provides clear guidelines about how to provide feedback about a student work sample. It also describes the concept of providing both "warm" and "cool" feedback in order to move beyond superficial comments.

Another way to discuss the positive and challenging aspects of a student assignment is to adapt a student feedback form for writing. Discuss what makes an assignment "glow" and where an assignment needs to "grow."

Grows and Glows

Student Name _____

Conference Date _____

Grows

_____

_____

_____

_____

Glows!

_____

_____

_____

_____

Try It Out!

Think about the five activities for PLCs. Brainstorm your ideas about how to use each in your own Professional Learning Community.

Activities for PLCs	*Your Ideas*
Book Studies	
Developing Consistent Expectations	
Learning Walks	
Lesson Studies	
Looking at Student Work	

10

Opportunities and Challenges

Now that you have a strong base of instructional strategies, let's turn our attention to the opportunities and challenges that lie ahead. In my workshops on rigor, teachers generally ask me five main questions.

Five Questions
- ♦ Where Should I Begin?
- ♦ How Do I Handle Resistance from Students?
- ♦ What Do I Say to Parents?
- ♦ How Should I Respond When Other Teachers Aren't Supportive?
- ♦ How Can I Gauge Progress?

Where Should I Begin?

By this point, you may be a bit overwhelmed. We've covered a tremendous amount of material in a short time. Ideally, you could snap your fingers and all of your students would immediately embrace more rigorous expectations and assignments. But the reality is that creating an environment in which each student is expected to learn at high levels, each student is supported so he or she can learn at high levels, and each student demonstrates learning at high levels is not easy. It takes time, consistency, and persistence.

Your first step is to have a vision of your classroom where all of those things occur. Turn back to the vision letter you wrote at the end of chapter 1, The Case for Rigor. Reread it, and revise it now that we are at the end of the book. Take your time and add as many details as possible. Describe fully how things have changed now that each student you teach learns at high levels. Then, read it at least once a week. Clarifying your vision and focusing on your vision are the foundations for your success.

Second, decide on three specific steps you will take to increase rigor in your classroom. We've discussed at least 25 in the preceding chapters, so you need to pick the ones that are most applicable to you. As you incorporate the new ideas, take time to reflect and make any adaptations. No idea is perfect; most will need some adjustments to be effective with your students. Then, continue to incorporate at least one new strategy or idea each week throughout the school year. As you slowly integrate changes into your instruction, you will create the vision you described in your letter.

It's Your Turn!

Review the strategies in chapters 4 through 8. Pick three specific ideas you would like to try in the next three weeks. Make those your top priority. Now, list any other specific activities you want to use later.

Top Three Ideas to Implement	Ideas to Try Later

How Do I Handle Resistance from Students?

Although it's not a certainty, it is likely that you will meet some resistance from students as you increase the rigor in your classroom. There are several possible reasons for this. Some students simply don't see the value of hard work. Others don't feel successful in school, and the thought of something that is even more difficult increases their fears of failure. While we can't solve every problem you face with your students, there are three recommendations that will help ease the transition to more rigorous work.

First, recognize the source of the resistance. The value and success aspects of motivation impact students in more ways than you may realize. As you create your lessons, tap into value from your students' perspective. In the early stages of planning, ask yourself "What will I say to a student who says, 'What's In It For Me?'" Integrate real world applications as much as possible. In order to help students feel successful, build in multiple opportunities for appropriate scaffolding and support.

Next, give your students time. Real change doesn't happen overnight. If your students grumble and complain, minimize the discussion, increase your focus on relevance and success, and keep moving forward. Celebrate their successes, large and small. Include positive reinforcement for reaching goals, but also for sustained effort toward a goal. Focus on the long-term effects of helping your students grow, and you will see a difference. And remember, it will probably take longer than you'd prefer, and your students won't always tell you that they appreciate what you do. My graduate students regularly joke about my classes, telling new students that "Dr. Blackburn's classes are appreciated more when they are over." That may be true for your classroom also.

Finally, although you need to be clear about what you are doing, don't give rigor too much of the spotlight. I talked with one teacher who said "When I created lessons that were highly interactive and engaging, made sure I incorporated the relevance for students, and showed them I would help them be successful, they quit complaining and realized this was just about learning!" Expect the best from your students, create the best lessons to ensure learning, provide appropriate support for every student, and don't apologize for your high standards.

It's Your Turn!

Which of the three recommendations will be most effective as you increase rigor in your classroom? Draft a plan below.

Recommendation	My Ideas
Recognize the source of resistance (value or success).	
Give students time to adjust.	
Share the spotlight.	

What Do I Say to Parents?

In addition to providing information for your students, you need to communicate effectively with parents. It's important to provide a clear description of what you expect. If your expectations are higher than other teachers, or if this is a new concept for parents, you will need to focus on your rationale and the benefits of rigor. It's certainly easier if everyone in your school is collaborating as you increase expectations, but if that isn't the case, then you simply need to ensure that parents understand why your requirements are different. Think about the two keys of motivation. Parents need to see value in what you are doing, and they need to feel they and their sons or daughters will be successful.

I recently spoke with a principal whose school slowly and steadily increased rigor across all grade levels and subject areas. However, a parent of a transfer student was concerned. At the former school, his daughter was a straight A student who had exerted little effort. She was still making As, but was having to invest more time and energy to do so. He was concerned that her schoolwork was "no longer easy for her. I don't want her to have to work too much. I want her to have fun." Rather than launching into an explanation of the importance of rigor, the principal asked about the student's educational goals. When the father responded that she would be attending college immediately out of high school, the principal then explained their philosophy on rigor, linking it to college level expectations (see chapter 1, The Case for Rigor). He tapped into the father's value and showed how the work his daughter was doing now would help her be successful in college.

Formula for Communication
Value + Success = Understanding

As I said in chapter 8, Assessment and Grading, I've found that providing information in writing is always beneficial. During the first two weeks of school, Kendra Alston guides her students as they create a brochure for parents about her classroom. "The students do all preliminaries, I just put it together. I tell them my philosophy; then each block gets together and comes up with a quote that describes their class. It also includes a poem I write to parents every year that finishes by asking for support from them. I always finish with the message that I can't do anything without you (parents)." She also informs them of basic information they need during the year, including her contact information, grading and homework information, and any other relevant classroom policies.

I also suggest you share information throughout the year. You can continue to use newsletters, but shift the focus to celebrating the progress students are making. You can take digital pictures of their writing or projects they have created. Incorporate their reflective comments about learning, using their comments to showcase growth. This can also help you balance an overemphasis on grades.

It's Your Turn!

What information do you need to share with parents? How would you like to share it?

General Suggestions	*Your Ideas*
Why is rigor valuable to the parents of your students?	
What information do you need to send home at the start of the year?	
How will you showcase your students' work throughout the year?	

Helping Parents Understand a "Not Yet" or "Instant Credit Recovery" Program

In chapter 8, we discussed a not yet grading policy. I also shared Toni Eubank's philosophy of "Instant Credit Recovery." If you or your school implements a similar policy, you are likely to hear something like this:

"Our school is one of the best in our area. As parents, we have high expectations, and if sons and daughters don't do the work, they receive a zero. Zeroes and failing grades prepare our students for real life."

There are many ways to explain why a policy which requires that students complete their work at a satisfactory level doesn't undermine teaching responsibility, but I'm going to share Toni's response. I think it's the best I've heard.

Life has many do-overs, and when parents think otherwise, they do not have a handle on the "real world" as it works today. Quality is the most important component of any job. Ask BP oil workers, their supervisors and even their now defunct CEOs. When due dates and dollars replace high-quality work, or even minimum standards, the results can be devastating. America was built on quality and innovation, and until and unless we instill these values into our students, they leave our schools with notions about "the real world" that do not actually exist in their lives. When I hear things like, "they won't get to redo work when they get on the job. They will have time-lines, and if they don't do the work, they will get fired." Actually, on the job, they will have a set of expectations and responsibilities that require them to do their work at high levels and they will have to redo that work until they get it right. If they are unable to do it to begin with, they will get extra help—a lot of extra help. If the job requires knowledge and skills they do not have, they will get on-the-job training, assistance and even a mentor until they are able to do the work. Some need longer training than others, but only the inept or lazy do not make it through. If they are still unable or unwilling, they will be notified of the need for improvement, usually more than once. In most jobs, they will get verbal, then written notification of the quality of their work and of what will need to happen in order to remain on the job. If they still do not meet the work standard, then and only then will those workers be fired. Few jobs require workers to do perfect, even high-quality, or even minimal work or be fired on the spot. There are steps in the firing process that must be followed.

Our current methods and the real values our schools teach students is the opposite of almost every real-world job. "If you don't do your work, you will get a zero," tells a student there is an *option* to do work or not. They can do the work *or* they can choose not to do the work. A zero is something that occurs in their future, and in this world, this generation works almost solely through instant gratification and instant consequences, students do not understand the impact of zeros, even when teachers try to tell them. (Eubank, 2011, p. 2–3)

How Should I Respond When Other Teachers Aren't Supportive?

Unfortunately, as you incorporate new ideas in your classroom, you may also meet resistance from other teachers in your school. Here's how a third-year teacher described his experience:

I do a lot of rigorous, interactive, and engaging activities that result in my students talking to their friends about what we do in class. Other social studies teachers heard about my classroom activities from their students. As a result the group of teachers who had taught much longer considered me an outsider and not a team player simply because of this, which made it virtually impossible to have any voice at grade level meetings. I was viewed as a troublemaker. Several colleagues did ask me about my activities and complimented me, and a couple of social studies teachers started doing some of the same activities. This also increased my negative ratings with those in power because I was spreading my troublesome ways of helping students learn and not conforming to tried and true strategies of talking for an hour and having kids copy notes or fill-in-the-blank worksheets.

I hope you never have to deal with a situation like this one, but my experience is that it happens more often than we think. I've spoken to too many teachers who have dealt with similar situations to assume this is the exception.

I think this is probably the most difficult challenge in terms of resistance. You would hope that the other teachers and administrators you work with would support you. But if you find that you are in a similar situation, there are two actions you can take to help you balance the negative criticism.

First, try to keep a lower profile. One of my former students was so excited about the changes she saw in her students; she enthusiastically shared her successes at every departmental meeting. The other teachers viewed this as bragging, and mistakenly perceived her excitement as arrogance. At the end of the first semester, she called me in tears, ready to change jobs. However, she was committed to her students, and wanted some advice. I suggested she limit the information she shared at meetings, waiting until she was asked about her ideas, and taking a more laid-back approach with other faculty. Periodically, she asked her department chair for advice on her lessons, to gain valuable feedback and to show respect for the teacher's experience and expertise. Through these actions, the other teachers were more responsive to her ideas, and she built a stronger working relationship with them. The following year, she was able to take a leadership role in a schoolwide reform effort.

Next, seek out other teachers with similar beliefs. One of the benefits of the graduate program at my former university is the support and friendship of other teachers. At graduation, I was regularly told by my students that one of the things they would miss most is the ability to come in and discuss issues with others who share similar perspectives about making a difference for students. It's easy to feel isolated when you are trying something new; find others who can support you. With the advent of technology, it's relatively easy to build your personal learning community.

Finally, remember your focus. The teacher in the above example told me, "High performance often leads to jealousy in the workplace. I suppose that's anywhere, except that in teaching it should be about the students." I agree. It is about the students. When you center your effort and attention on what is best for your students, it helps you balance the criticism from others. One of the most effective ways to keep yourself motivated in tough times is to keep a daily list of five positive things that happen with your students. Then, when you have a bad day, you can look back at the list to help you remember that you are making a difference.

It's Your Turn!

Keeping a "Positives List" helps you keep your perspective, whether you are dealing with resistance from other teachers, or just having a bad week. Try it for one week and see if it makes a difference. For a template of a "Positives List," please visit www.routledge.com/9781596672260.

How Can I Gauge Progress?

One of the most frustrating aspects of teaching is determining if you are making progress. Verifying that based on the number of student or parent complaints is probably not the best gauge. It's important to remember that creating a classroom culture that is rigorous will take time, and you may experience plateaus. However, rubrics can help us assess our progress. I've broken down the rubric starting on p. 161 into seven criteria: the three elements from our definition, student engagement, the two keys to motivation, and overall classroom culture. A more printer-friendly version of this rubric and the self-assessment chart on page 166 can be downloaded from:

Rubric for Gauging Progress Toward Rigor

	Starting at the Base	Making Progress Up the Mountain	Reaching New Heights
High Expectations for Learning	I am working to understand what it means to say that each student can learn, will learn, and I will help them do so.	I believe that each student can learn, will learn, and I will help them do so. I sometimes act on those beliefs or I act on those beliefs with some students.	I consistently act on my unwavering belief that each student can learn, will learn, and I will help them do so.
Support and Scaffolding	I sometimes provide support and scaffolding. This support is usually general and built into the regular lesson. At times, I provide optional extra help.	I sometimes provide the appropriate support and scaffolding students need to ensure their success. This support is customized for each student at times. At times, I provide optional extra help.	I regularly provide the support and scaffolding each student needs to ensure their success. This support is customized for each student and supports my belief that students are not allowed to not learn. It is appropriate and encourages independence. If extra help is needed, it is required, and is offered when the student can attend.

(continued)

Rubric for Gauging Progress Toward Rigor (cont'd)

	Starting at the Base	Making Progress Up the Mountain	Reaching New Heights
Demonstration of Learning	Occasionally, some students demonstrate understanding of content in a way that is appropriately challenging. More often than not, students prefer basic assignments or questions. Students are generally given one opportunity to show they have mastered content.	Sometimes, students are given the opportunity to show they understand content in a way that is appropriately challenging. Students are beginning to see the value of more challenging assessments. At times, I provide alternative assessments and will allow students to redo work.	Each student regularly demonstrates their understanding of content in ways that are appropriately challenging. In other words, students do not take the easy way out in terms of showing me they learned. I provide alternative ways for students to do this and allow those students who need it extra time or a second opportunity.

(continued)

Rubric for Gauging Progress Toward Rigor (cont'd)

	Starting at the Base	Making Progress Up the Mountain	Reaching New Heights
Level of Student Engagement	There are limited opportunities for students to be engaged in learning beyond listening and taking notes. Most of my instruction is directed toward the whole class. At times, I provide the opportunity for students to work with another student to apply their learning.	Some students are actively engaged in learning. There is a mix of whole group and small group/partner activities, and some activities are interactive. I facilitate some activities, and some ownership is shifted to students. However, the focus is still on me.	All students are actively engaged in learning. Each is participating in every aspect of the lesson by making connections, contributing to the discussion (whether small group, partner, or whole group), and responding to learning. The majority of the activities are interactive, and whole group activities are limited. I am the facilitator, and the focus for learning is on the students.

(continued)

Opportunities and Challenges ◆ 163

Rubric for Gauging Progress Toward Rigor (cont'd)

	Starting at the Base	*Making Progress Up the Mountain*	*Reaching New Heights*
Motivational Element: Value	I ask students to apply my lessons to their real lives. I make sure my students understand how my lesson applies to future tests they will take (such as standardized testing). I sometimes share with them why I think the content is important.	I sometimes design lessons that allow students to see the value. I incorporate real-life application activities into some of my lessons. If they volunteer, students can share their own applications of learning.	I design lessons that allow students to see the value of the specific learning. Application activities are woven seamlessly throughout the lesson. Students are given ample opportunity to make personal connections about relevance to their own lives and futures.
Motivational Element: Success	If the majority of my students aren't learning, I reteach the content of the lesson. Sometimes, I provide opportunities for students to come in for extra help if they want to. I expect my students to succeed, and I am learning how to help them understand that.	I build scaffolding into some lessons. I provide opportunities for students to come in for extra help when needed. I regularly tell my students that I expect them to succeed, and I try to help them make that a reality.	I build appropriate scaffolding and support into every lesson. Students know my focus is to remove barriers to their success. I require students to come in for extra help when needed, and I support them in positive ways that encourage growth and independent learning. All students know that we learn together, and that they can be successful.

(continued)

Rubric for Gauging Progress Toward Rigor (cont'd)

	Starting at the Base	Making Progress Up the Mountain	Reaching New Heights
Overall Classroom Culture	Members of our learning community (students, teachers, parents, etc.) are learning what it means to set a standard that **not learning** is unacceptable. We are also discussing how to move beyond grades to authentic learning. We celebrate some of our successes.	Some members of our learning community (students, teachers, parents, etc.) believe that it is unacceptable **to not learn.** We are learning to focus on learning in addition to grades. We celebrate success as well as progress.	Every member of our learning community (students, teachers, parents, etc.) believes that it is unacceptable **to not learn.** The focus is on learning at high levels, not just grades. We celebrate success as well as progress.

As you look at the descriptions, remember this is a journey, much like climbing a mountain. You may be discouraged if you think you are at the base, looking at how far you need to climb. Don't be. Everyone has to start somewhere, and I've always found that when I'm at the bottom, that means I have nowhere to go but up! Increasing the rigor in your classroom is about making progress, one step at a time. If you stay positive and keep moving forward, you will reach new heights with your students.

It's Your Turn!

Think about where you are right now. Use the blank rubric to self-assess your classroom or school. For each criterion, mark your current status. A more printer-friendly version of this chart can be downloaded from: www.routledge.com/9781596672260.

	Starting at the Base	*Making Progress Up the Mountain*	*Reaching New Heights*
High Expectations for Learning			
Support and Scaffolding			
Demonstration of Learning			
Level of Student Engagement			
Motivational Element: Value			
Motivational Element: Success			
Overall Classroom Culture			

Now, make plans for ways to improve in each area.

	Steps to Improve
High Expectations for Learning	
Support and Scaffolding	
Demonstration of Learning	
Level of Student Engagement	
Motivational Element: Value	
Motivational Element: Success	
Overall Classroom Culture	

Conclusion

When you choose to raise expectations and increase the rigor of your classroom, you are choosing a path that is likely to include some storms. Throughout this book, I've focused on specific actions you can take in your own classroom. As I was finishing the last chapter, a superintendent told me, "In my district, we believe the best way to increase rigor is through a realignment of curriculum for our courses." In chapter 1, The Case for Rigor, you may remember there is research to support that as a key method for increasing rigor. He then asked why I didn't focus the entire book on the curriculum aspect. It's simple. I meet many teachers who are told they are to teach their current curriculum without changes. Those teachers say to me, "If I have to teach what I'm given, is there anything I can do to increase rigor?"

I believe the answer is a resounding "yes." I've purposely placed the spotlight on what happens within your classroom, the actions that are within your control as a teacher. If you are one teacher trying to make a difference within your classroom, you have a treasure box of resources at your disposal.

In chapter 1, The Case for Rigor, we read comments from students describing their perspectives of rigor. Before we finish, I'd like to leave you with some additional thoughts from them. My second question was, "What would you tell a teacher who wants to increase rigor in his or her classroom?"

Students' Recommendations to Teachers

- Teach us how to do it in an easy way. *Allen*
- Don't give us too much. *Destiny*
- Help me when I don't know how. *Jeremy*
- Make sure you know how to do it if you want me to do it. *Pario*
- Make it fun! *Chandler*
- Don't go through things so fast you forget what was taught. *Nikki*
- Teach us something we have not learned. *Akia*
- Don't overload us, but do a little at a time. *Brendowlen*
- It's alright with me, as long as I can get help when I need it after I have already tried it. *Lindsay*
- Don't be discouraged if some of your students think that it is hard because it's supposed to be hard. *Kevin*

As a final note, there is an African Proverb that says, "Smooth seas do not make skillful sailors." You will likely encounter some difficulties along the way. True learning is an adventure, and I've always found my most powerful lessons came when an experience did not go as planned. My hope for you and your students is that, as you encounter those unexpected moments, you reflect, learn from them, and adjust and improve together. Then, when you finish the journey, you will find you are stronger than when you began.

Final Insights

- The most important idea I read was . . .

- One way I plan to apply this information in my classroom is . . .

- I wonder . . .

Correlations to the Common Core State Standards For English Language Arts

Grades K–12

Classroom Strategy	Anchor Standards for English Language Arts, Grades K–12
Chapter 2: Digging Into Rigor	
Design a Game, p. 30	SL.4
	SL.5
	L.6
Chapter 3: Raise the Level of Content	
Book Webs, p. 36	R.9
	SL.1
	SL.2
	SL.4
	SL.5
Follow-up Articles, p. 40	R.9
	SL.1
	SL.2
	SL.4
Limited Choice, p. 42	R.10
Pair Texts, p. 42	R.9
	W.7
	W.8
	W.9
Sample Renaissance Unit, p. 44	R.1
	R.2
	R.7
	W.3
	W.7
	SL.5
	L.6
Create a Classified Ad, p. 46	L.1
	L.5

Classroom Strategy	Anchor Standards for English Language Arts, Grades K–12
Folder Game, p. 47	R.1
	R.2
	R.9
	W.2
	W.5
	W.10
	SL.1
	L.1
	L.2
Students Teach Each Other, p. 48	SL.1
	SL.6
Chapter 4: Increase Complexity	
Show Me What You Know, p. 54	R.7
	R.9
	R.10
	W.7
	W.8
	W.9
	SL.4
	SL.5
	SL.6
Answer Your Own Question, p. 55	W.7
Discover Purposes for Cheerios, p. 55	SL.1
	SL.2
RAFT Strategy for Rigor in Writing, p. 56	W.2
	W.4
	W.6
	W.8

Classroom Strategy	Anchor Standards for English Language Arts, Grades K–12
	W.10
Correct the Quiz, p. 58	W.5
	W.9
	W.10
	SL.1
Create an Alphabet of Math Terms, p. 58	L.6
Share Ideas, p. 58	W.2
	W.5
	W.10
	SL.1
	SL.3
Predictions Using Words, p. 59	SL.1
	L.6
Vocabulary Chart, p. 61	L.4
	L.5
	L.6
What Am I? Riddles, p. 62	W.10
	L.4
	L.5
	L.6
Question Review Games, p. 65	W.9
	W.10
	SL.1
	SL.5
	L.1
	L.2
	L.6

Classroom Strategy	Anchor Standards for English Language Arts, Grades K–12
Chapter 5: Give Appropriate Support and Guidance	
Guide-O-Rama, p. 70	R.1
	R.2
	R.3
	R.4
	R.5
	R.7
	R.10
	SL.5
	L.4
	L.6
Interactive Reading Guide, p. 71	R.1
	R.2
	R.3
	R.9
	W.1
	W.6
	W.7
	W.8
	SL.1
	SL.2
	SL.5
Math Graphic Organizer, p. 72	R.1
	R.4
	W.2
	W.10
	SL.5
	L.4

Classroom Strategy	Anchor Standards for English Language Arts, Grades K–12
	L.6
Layering Meaning, p. 73	R.1
	R.2
	R.9
	R.10
Model Expected Instructional Behaviors, p. 74	R.5
	SL.2
	L.4
	L.6
Providing Clear Expectations, p. 76	R.1
	W.4
	W.5
	SL.1
	SL.2
	SL.3
	R.9
	R.10
	W.4
	W.5
	W.7
	W.8
	W.9
	W.10
	SL.1
Presenting Multiple Opportunities to Learn, p. 80	R.10
	SL.1
	SL.2
	SL.6

Classroom Strategy	Anchor Standards for English Language Arts, Grades K–12
Chapter 6: Open Your Focus	
Open-Ended Questioning, p. 87	R.1
	R.3
	SL.1
	L.5
Open-Ended Research, p. 90	R.9
	W.2
	W.3
	W.4
	W.7
	W.8
	W.9
	SL.1
	SL.2
	SL.4
	SL.5
	SL.6
Open-Ended Vocabulary Instruction, p. 93	W.10
	SL.1
	L.3
	L.5
	L.6
Roller Coaster Rigor, p. 96	W.2
	W.4
	W.10
	SL.1
	SL.2
	SL.4

Classroom Strategy	Anchor Standards for English Language Arts, Grades K–12
	SL.5
Musical-Rhythmic Social Studies Project, p. 97	R.2
	R.4
	R.9
	W.2
	W.4
	W.6
	W.7
	W.8
	W.10
	SL.4
	SL.5
Verbal-Linguistic Social Studies Project, p. 97	R.2
	R.9
	W.10
	SL.6
Visual-Spatial Social Studies Project, p. 98	R.1
	R.3
	R.10
	W.7
	W.8
	W.9
	W.10
	SL.4
	SL.5
	SL.6
Bodily-Kinesthetic Social Studies Project, p. 98	W.2
	W.7

Classroom Strategy	Anchor Standards for English Language Arts, Grades K–12
	W.9
	W.10
	SL.4
	SL.5
	SL.6
Advertisement for Chinese Invention, p. 100	W.1
	W.7
	W.8
	W.9
	W.10
Language Arts Project, p. 100	W.1
	W.3
	W.4
	SL.1
	SL.2
	SL.4
	SL.6
Math Project, p. 100	SL.2
	SL.4
	SL.5
	L.6
Science Project, p. 100	W.1
	W.9
	SL.1
	SL.2
	SL.4
	SL.5
	SL.6

Classroom Strategy	Anchor Standards for English Language Arts, Grades K–12
Social Studies Project, p. 101	W.1
	W.9
	SL.1
	SL.4
	SL.6
Band Project, p. 101	SL.2
Career/Technology Project, p. 101	W.3
	W.4
	W.6
	W.7
	W.8
	W.9
	W.10
Tic-Tac-Toe Interview, p. 104	R.7
	W.2
	W.4
	W.5
	W.7
	W.10
	SL.4
	SL.5
Tic-Tac-Toe Mystery Packet of Math Problems, p. 104	R.7
	W.8
	SL.5
	L.6
Tic-Tac-Toe Graph Booklet, p. 104	R.7
	W.2
	W.7

Classroom Strategy	Anchor Standards for English Language Arts, Grades K–12
	W.10
	SL.5
	L.6
Tic-Tac-Toe Calendar, p. 104	SL.5
Tic-Tac-Toe Crossword Puzzle, p. 104	R.4
	R.10
	W.4
	L.6
Tic-Tac-Toe Medals Graph, p. 104	R.7
	W.8
	SL.4
	SL.5
Tic-Tac-Toe Misleading Advertisements Booklet, p. 104	R.1
	R.7
	R.8
	R.10
	W.2
	W.4
	W.7
	W.8
	W.10
	SL.4
	SL.5
Tic-Tac-Toe Box and Whisker Plots, p. 104	R.7
	W.7
	W.8
	SL.4
	SL.5

Classroom Strategy	Anchor Standards for English Language Arts, Grades K–12
	L.6
Tic-Tac-Toe Discovering Algebra, p. 104	R.1
	R.10
	SL.4
	SL.5
Chapter 7: Raise Expectations	
T-Shirt Project, p. 113	W.2
	W.4
	W.7
	W.8
	W.9
	W.10
	SL.5
Theme Song, p. 113	W.4
	W.10
Vision Letter, Poster, Folder p. 114	W.2
	W.4
	W.10
	SL.4
Banned Book Persuasive Letter, p. 117	W.1
	W.4
	W.10
	SL.1
	SL.2
	SL.3
Students As Teachers, p. 118	SL.1
	SL.2
	SL.4

Classroom Strategy	Anchor Standards for English Language Arts, Grades K–12
	SL.6
School As a Business, p. 118	W.10
	SL.1
	SL.2
Reflective Writing to Track Progress, p. 120	W.2
	W.4
	W.10
Victory List, p. 120	W.2
	W.4
	W.10
Stop and Go Reflection, p. 121	W.2
	W.4
	W.10
Student-Led Conference, p. 121	SL.1
	SL.2
	SL.4
	SL.6
Chapter 8: Assessment and Grading	
Instant Credit Recovery, p. 136	W.5
Not Yet Grading, p. 137	W.5
Reassessment/Retaking of Tests, p. 137	W.2
	W.4
	W.5
	W.9
	W.10
Chapter 10: Opportunities and Challenges	
Brochure for Parents, p. 156	W.2
	W.4

Classroom Strategy	Anchor Standards for English Language Arts, Grades K–12
	W.10
	SL.1
	SL.2
	SL.4
	SL.5
	SL.6

References

Achieve. (2010). *Achieving the possible: What Americans think about the college- and career-ready agenda*. Washington, D.C.: Author.

Achieve. (2011). *State college- and career-ready high school graduation requirements*. Washington, D.C.: Author.

Achieve. (2011). *Closing the expectations gap 2011*. Washington, D.C.: Author.

ACT. (2011). *The condition of college- and career-readiness*. Iowa City, Iowa: Author.

Ainsworth, L. (2011) *Rigorous curriculum design: How to create curricular units of study that align standards, instruction, and assessment*. Lanham, MD: Advanced Learning Press.

Anderson, L. W., Krathwohl, D. R., Airasian, P. W., Cruikshank, K. A., Mayer, R. E., Pintrich, P. R., et al. (Eds.) (2001). *A taxonomy for learning, teaching, and assessing: A revision of Bloom's taxonomy of educational objectives*. New York: Longman.

Barrell, J. (2007). *Problem-based learning: An inquiry approach, 2nd edition*. Thousand Oaks, California: Corwin Press.

Beane, J. (2001). *Rigor and relevance: Can we have our cake and eat it too?* Paper presented at the Annual Conference of the National Middle School Association, Washington.

Benjamin, A. (2008). *Formative assessment for English language arts*. Larchmont, NY: Eye On Education.

Black, P., Harrison, C., Lee, C., Marshall, B., & Wiliam D. (2004). Working inside the black box: Assessment for learning in the classroom. *Phi Delta Kappan, 86*, 9–21.

Blackburn, B. R. (2005). *Classroom motivation from A to Z: How to engage your students in learning*. Larchmont, NY: Eye On Education.

Blackburn, B. R. (2007). *Classroom instruction from A to Z: How to promote student learning*. Larchmont, NY: Eye On Education.

Blackburn, B. and Williamson, R. (2010). *Four myths of rigor* [White paper]. Retrieved from. http://www.eyeoneducation.com/Online-Resources/White-Papers.

Blackburn, B. (2011). *Common Core State Standards: Only the beginning* [White paper]. Retrieved from http://www.eyeoneducation.com/Online-Resources/White-Papers.

Blackburn, B. (2012). *Rigor made easy: Getting started*. Larchmont, NY: Eye On Education.

Bottoms, G. and Timberlake A. (2011). *Preparing middle school students for success: A comparative study of most-and least-improved middle grades schools.* Atlanta, GA: Southern Regional Education Board.

Carmichael, S., Wilson, S., Porter-Magee, K., and Martino, G. (2010). *The State of State Standards—and the Common Core—in 2010.* Washington, DC: Thomas B. Fordham Institute.

Center on Education Policy. (2012). *Year two of implementing the common core state standards: States' progress and challenges.* Washington, D.C.: Author.

Ciardiello, A. V. (1998). Did you ask a good question today? Alternative cognitive and metacognitive strategies. *Journal of Adolescent & Adult Literacy, 42,* 210–220.

Colvin, R. and Jacobs, J. (2010). *Rigor: It's all the rage, but what does it mean?* New York: Teachers College at Columbia University.

Diller, D. (2007). *Making the most of small groups: Differentiation for all.* Portland, ME: Stenhouse.

DuFour, Ri, DuFour, Re, Easker, R. and Many, T. (2006). *Learning by doing: A handbook for professional learning communities at work.* Bloomington, IN: Solution Tree.

Eubank, T. SREB. Instant credit recovery or instant "content" recovery for middle grades: ICR Summary and implementation strategies. (unpublished white paper). Accessed January 3, 2011.

Fielding, L. & Roller, C. (1992, May). Making difficult books accessible and easy books acceptable. *The Reading Teacher,* 678–685.

Fisher, D., Frey, N., and Lapp, D. (2012). *Text complexity: Raising rigor in reading.* Newark, DE: International Reading Association.

Gardner, H. (1983). *Frames of mind: The theory of multiple intelligences.* New York: Basic Books.

Guskey, T. R., & Bailey, J. M. (2001). *Developing grading and reporting systems for student learning.* Thousand Oaks, CA: Corwin Press.

Lindsay, J. and Davis, V. (2013). *Flattening classrooms, engaging minds: Move to global collaboration one step at a time.* Boston, MA: Pearson.

Marzano, R. J. (2007). *The art of science and teaching: A comprehensive framework for effective instruction.* Alexandria, VA: Association for Supervision and Curriculum Development.

National Commission on Excellence in Education. (1983). *A nation at risk: The imperative for educational reform.* Washington, D.C.: U.S. Department of Education.

National Governors Association Center for Best Practices, Council of Chief State School Officers (2010). *The Common Core state standards for English language arts.* Washington D.C.: National Governors Association Center for Best Practices, Council of Chief State School Officers.

No Child Left Behind (NCLB) Act of 2001, Pub. L. No. 107-110, §1208, 115, Stat. 1550, 1551 (2002). Retrieved November 12, 2007 from http://www. ed. gov

O'Conner, K. (2002). *How to grade for learning: Linking grades to standards.* Thousand Oaks, CA: Corwin Press.

Olge, D. (1986). K-W-L: A teaching model that develops active reading of expository text. *Reading Teacher, 39,* 564–571.

Popham, W. J. (2008). *Transformative assessment.* Alexandria, VA: Association for Supervision and Curriculum Development.

Santa, C., Havens, L., & Macumber, E. (1996). *Creating independence through student-owned strategies.* Dubuque, IA: Kendall/Hunt.

Schlechty, P. (2011). *Engaging students: The next level of working on the work.* San Francisco, CA: Jossey-Bass.

Smerdon, B. and Borman, K., eds. (2012). *Pressing forward: Increasing and expanding rigor and relevance in America's high school.* Charlotte, NC: Information Age Publishing.

Southern Regional Education Board. (2010). *Broadening the definition of rigor for instructional improvement and academic achievement.* Jacksonville Florida TCTW National Forum. Atlanta, Georgia: Author.

Stanley, T. (2012). *Project-based learning for gifted students: A handbook for the 21st century classroom.* Waco, Texas: Prufrock Press.

Strong, R. W., Silver, H. F., & Perrini, M. J. (2001). *Teaching what matters most: Standards and strategies for raising student achievement.* Alexandria, VA: Association for Supervision and Curriculum Development.

Tovani, C. (2011). *So what do they really know? Assessment that informs teaching and learning.* Portland, ME: Stenhouse.

Wagner, T. (2006). Rigor on trial. *Education Week.* Retrieved April 13, 2008, from http://www.gse.harvard.edu/clg/pdfs/rigorontrialedweek.pdf

Wiederhold, C. (1995). *Cooperative learning and higher level thinking: The Q-matrix.* San Clemente, CA: Kagan.

Williamson, R. and Blackburn, B. (2010). *Rigorous schools and classrooms: Leading the way.* Larchmont, NY: Eye On Education.

Williamson, R. and Blackburn, B. (2011). *Rigor in your school: A toolkit for leaders.* Larchmont, NY: Eye On Education.

Wyatt, J., Wiley, A., Camara, W., and Proestler, N. (2011). *The development of an index of academic rigor for college readiness.* Washington, D.C.: The College Board.

Notes

Notes

Notes

Notes

Notes